The
Book
of
Yaak

RICK BASS

A Mariner Book
Houghton Mifflin Company
BOSTON · NEW YORK

The
Book
of
Yaak

For information about permission to reproduce selections from
this book, write to Permissions, Houghton Mifflin Company,
215 Park Avenue South, New York, New York 10003.

Library of Congress Cataloging-in-Publication Data
Bass, Rick.
  The book of Yaak / Rick Bass.
    p. cm.
  ISBN 0-395-77014-9   ISBN 0-395-87746-6 (pbk.)
  1. Nature conservation—Montana—Yaak Valley.
  2. Nature. 3. Yaak Valley (Mont.). I. Title.
QH76.5.M9B37   1996
508.786'81—dc20   96-27270 CIP

Printed in the United States of America

QUM 10 9 8 7 6 5

The author is grateful to the Lyndhurst Foundation and to the
following magazines, which first published some of these essays
in different form: *Steelhead, Wild Duck Review, Orion, House
Beautiful, AFSEE (Association of Forest Service Employees for
Environmental Ethics), Montana Magazine, Audubon, Sierra,
Sports Afield, Big Sky Journal, Southern Review, Eugene Weekly,
Sonora Review,* and the anthologies *Best American Nature Writ-
ing 1994* and *Best American Nature Writing 1996.*

Contents

Introduction   *xiii*

Home   *1*

The Value of a Place   *2*

Almost Like Hibernation   *14*

The Land That Congress Forgot   *21*

Four Coyotes   *28*

The Fringe   *37*

My Grizzly Story   *45*

Antlers   *59*

Waterfall   *66*

The Music and Harmony
of Large and Small Things   *67*

Winter Coyotes   *86*

The Blood Root of Art   *87*

The Storekeeper   *95*

Cores   *101*

The Dark-Eyed Owls   *113*

This Savage Land   *123*

Healing   136

Fires   140

My Congressman   150

Hot Lead   152

The Totem Pole   171

Metamorphosis   174

Conclusion   188

As we destroy that which is natural
we eat ourselves alive.

—*William Kittredge*

Introduction

I SHIVER, AS I WRITE THIS.

I'm shivering because it's winter in my windowless un-
heated rat-shed of a writing cabin.

I'm shivering because I'm so nakedly, openly, revealing
the earned secrets of my valley — places and things I know,
which the valley — the Yaak — has entrusted to me.

There is a place, a sanctuary you go to, in writing fiction,
or, I suppose, poetry, that is in another world. You are not in
control — and upon emerging from it, the writing of and the
inhabiting of that place, you feel new energy, new understanding. You've touched mystery.

It's magic. There's no other word for it — no way known to
explain it.

That's what I like to chase, or move toward: that feeling,
that place. It does try to escape.

This book is not like that. It's a sourcebook, a handbook, a
weapon of the heart. To a literary writer, it's a sin, to ask
something of the reader, rather than to give; and to know the
end, to know your agenda, from the very start, rather than
discovering it along the way, or at the end itself.

My valley is on fire — my valley is burning. It has been on
fire for over twenty years. These essays — these pleas to act to
save it — it's all I know how to do. I don't know if a book can
help protect a valley, and the people who live in that valley. I
know that a book can harm these things — that in our acquisitive culture, now that big business has us where they

want us — having advertised into us the notion that we want things and lots of them, and that we want the Best, the most Unique, the Ten Least Known — that a revelation of this valley's wild faint secrets could draw acquisitive sorts — those who come to the valley to take something, rather than give.

It is not a place to come to.

It is a place to save — a place to exercise our strength and compassion — that last little bit that the advertisers have not yet been able to breed, or condition, out of us.

This valley still exists in the Lower Forty-eight as a chance to explain to corporate America — Big Timber, mostly — that as human beings we still have at our core an essence, a yearning for and affiliation with wilderness, and that we can only be pushed and herded so far.

What do I want?

I want the last few roadless areas in this still-wild valley to remain that way.

I am not "against" logging — though I am against any more clearcuts in the valley. Too often the opposition paints tree huggers such as myself into total obstructionists.

I'm not writing this like any of my other books — certainly not like my novel. This is not really a book. This is instead an artifact of the woods, like a chunk of rhyolite, a shed deer antler, a bear skull, a heron feather.

I am convinced that anyone who hears the message of Yaak, logger and tree hugger alike, will agree that its wildness should be protected from corporate America. I am convinced the Yaak — 471,000 acres, of which only about 150,000 remain roadless — can be saved. It never has been saved before — inertia rules — but I do not believe inertia can rule forever.

I shiver, for these are the same words — the precise words — one finds in the third-class mailings for every other so-just cause both at home and abroad. Invariably, in all of these causes, the children are the ones who will pay most severely. The causes stun the mind with their commonness, their prevalence — their ubiquitousness. The mind, for balm's sake, recoils from them, files them immediately in some other empty, nonacquiring, nongiving part of the brain, and often turns to art — to a book, or music, or a painting — to calm the adrenaline spike, or the soul's stab.

If action cannot be roused on behalf of the handful of wolves hanging on in the Yaak Valley, or the handful of grizzlies, or the lone woodland caribou, or the last twelve pairs of bull trout, or the orchids and moonworts, sedges and swans — perhaps action can be roused by anger of what is being done to you, in secret. It is the dark story of America — the story of coal thugs and goons in Appalachia, the story of company towns, the story of intolerance, the story of the quick buck unraveling the hope for a sustainable future.

The wolves, the swans, the bears, are waiting patiently. I am convinced that the only way to save ourselves is to save the Yaak Valley. You may roll your eyes heavenward and put the book — the artifact — aside at such a statement, and if you do, I have failed the wolverines and the bears, have failed my neighbor Jesse who carves totem poles, five or six a year, out of fallen fir trees; failed my friends who trap and tan hides and sew them into buckskin (to sell sometimes to movie companies and actors and actresses who then film commercials advertising products owned by subsidiaries of the oil and timber companies whose products we use and who are bent on rubbing out the last roadless areas, the last wild places . . .).

We need wildness to protect us from ourselves.

We need wilderness to buffer this dark lost-gyroscopic tumble that democracy, top-heavy with big business and leaning precariously over rot, has entered.

We're an adolescent country, a tough, macho, posturing Madison Avenue sleek-jawed Marlboro Man's caricature of strength.

We need the strength of lilies, ferns, mosses and mayflies. We need the masculinity of ponds and rivers, the femininity of stone, the wisdom of quietness, if not silence.

For thirty years, the agencies — chiefly the U.S. Forest Service — and industries in command of this secret scandal have, year after year, uttered the platitudes "We're changing," and "We were bad then, before we knew any better, but now we're good, we're committed," and "Every day is Earth Day."

Every day in Montana, and the West, is big industry's Rip-Off Day. They're stripping public resources, public lands, faster than they can recover, and they're stripping away mystery.

Here is a chronicling, an accounting, of some of the things and places that are getting scraped clean.

The
Book
of
Yaak

Home

YAAK IS THE KOOTENAI WORD for arrow and it is the name of the valley where I live. The Kootenai once hunted in the upper part of the valley, the place where my cabin is now.

Those of us who live here now hunt through the ice for fish in January, hunt deer and elk in the snows of November, grouse in the blazing autumn; we gather berries in August, and tend to our gardens in the brief summer. We hunt firewood; we hunt mushrooms. We hunt for the deer's dropped antlers; we hunt for fir boughs for Christmas wreaths; we hunt a duck or two; and we hunt flat rocks for our rock walls. We hunt daisies and asters and lupine and paintbrush for our children in June. We hunt horses that have slipped through buck-and-rail fences knocked askew like toothpicks by night-passing moose.

Three couples up here trap and tan hides. There are three preachers; two bars. A handful of hunting and fishing guides. We do seasonal work, rhythmic work — planting trees in the spring to try to regenerate the scabrous clearcuts; we saw roadside lodgepole blowdown for firewood, and hundred-inch studs, to cart to Libby or Bonners Ferry in the backs of our beat-up pickups.

The people who live here — who stay here — have fallen in love with the shape of this land. Its cycle of days.

The Value of a Place

ALMOST AS BAD AS a writer asking for something, rather than giving, is the sin of repeating one's self, like some tired spit-dribbling codger at Christmas dinner telling that same damn story.

I wrote a book, *Winter*, which was about falling in love with this valley. I long for that innocence and suppleness of heart. Forgive me for repeating this one story, of how I stumbled into this place, but what was part of that old story — falling in love with, and learning to fit a place — is also part of this new story, which is about, I suppose, the second part of my cycle: the moon that must always answer to the sun — the giving back, after so much taking.

We wanted to be artists — my wife and I. Or rather, she was an artist, and I was a geologist and wanted to become instead a writer. I knew it would be hard to do both — geology and writing, science and art.

We left Mississippi when we were twenty-nine — in my old truck with our two hounds, who were only puppies then, and headed West, were pulled west, as seems to be the genetic predisposition in our country's blood — the handwriting of it telling us to move across the country from right to left, always farther from some echo of England, perhaps, or farther from everything — something in our blood and perhaps in the country beneath us that whispers for us always to rebel, even if only mildly — and that was what we did; we ran, for both the thrill of flight and for the searching-for-a-place.

All over the west we drove — we knew we loved mountains, loved rocks and ice and forests and creeks, loved sky and smoke — and we traveled through July thunderstorms and August snowstorms until one day we came over a pass and a valley appeared beneath us, a blue-green valley hidden beneath heavy clouds, with smoke rising from a couple of chimneys far below, and a lazy river snaking its way through the valley's narrow center, and a power, an immensity, that stopped us in our tracks. It was perhaps like the feeling of traveling a deep ocean while dragging an anchor, the anchor catching on something far below. It was the gravity of the place that caught my heart — that caught our hearts.

It took us a long time to settle in, to fit in, but not as long as it would have taken had we moved to yet another city, I don't believe. The move wasn't seamless, to say the least — I didn't even own a coat, or long underwear, for instance (Mississippi!) — but there was a match, right from the very start. I was starving for a thing but until then I had not realized what it was — and still, even as I discovered it, did not know the name of it, *peace* — though I knew that this valley had it, and would offer it to me, would let me feast upon it as if it were a meal: as if it were the sum of some strange combination of rock and forest and river that spoke only to our hearts — though I think it is safe to say that it speaks to the hearts of all those who have committed to living here: the whole hundred or so of us.

Is it too much to imagine that the pulsings of our blood, and our emotions, follow the rough profile of the days of light in this valley? the short summers of long days followed by the long winters of short days? the play of light in these strange forests, and even the sound of its creeks, somehow a place and sound that has almost always existed, which mirrors the sounds and rhythms inside us? Not a direct overlay, but a predisposition, so that our settling in was not so much work and effort as it was relief, pleasure and peace.

Does such a place exist for everyone?

How many places are left in the world — what diversity of them still exists — and for that diversity, what tolerance, and what affinity?

If a place is peaceful, can it impart that peace to its inhabitants — and if so, then how far — like a stone dropped into a pond — can that peace be spread?

What is the value of a place?

I wrote, and Elizabeth painted. I wrote in a place that was half-greenhouse, half-root-cellar — half submerged in the rich black earth, like a bear in hibernation, dreaming, yet also half immersed in light and surrounded by the scent and flavor of growing things — and Elizabeth painted out in the bright sun and wind, after that first winter had passed: painted scarves of bright colors, and bright landscapes.

We took, and took, and took. We feasted.

I can't tell you when the blinders of art, only art, first lifted: at what precise point I looked beyond the immediate visual reaction of what was being done to the country — the surgical incisions of the clearcuts, the scalpings — and felt the unease, or dis-ease, deeply enough to begin acting, or trying to act, against it. I'm not sure at which point I allowed the pain of it to be absorbed by me deeply enough so that I had no choice but to react against it. The clearcuts were never attractive, but for at least a year or two they did not touch me or harm me, nor my belief in peace, the way they do now — as does the threat of those clearcuts yet to come: those in the planning stages, and those that will come still later.

There had to be some point, though — some moment, some place, where something in me reached saturation — where I could not accept the sight of it anymore, and the knowledge of what the roads and clearcuts were doing to the ecology of the valley as well as to the economy of man. Undoubtedly this feeling of pain, of saturation, came at some point after I had gone through a full cycle of the four seasons;

perhaps after I had gone through them a couple of times. I moved through the woods on hikes and hunts, open-minded — I had heard that the clearcuts were sometimes beneficial for the production of summer browse for deer (never mind that the deer populations might then rise beyond the limitations of their winter range). There still seemed to be plenty of diversity in the forest types I saw, and the roadless cores — the sanctuaries — still seemed intact.

That was just over a decade ago. I'm not sure when I began to realize that they — the timber industry — wanted it all: or if not all of it immediately, then access to all of it, forever. Or as the occasional bumper sticker declared, "Wilderness = Land of No Use."

Each season, I picked up the feel and taste of cycles. My blood began to learn new rhythms. My body became increasingly fluent in the language of cycles: splitting wood on cold mornings, cleaning a grouse in the evening — the solace, and ceremony, of plucking the feathers. Noticing where elk foraged in summer and where they foraged in winter. Noticing where the bears fed and what they ate. Watching the pulse of different creeks and the Yaak River itself — skinny in autumn, icy but poised in winter — wild, joyful and enormous in spring, then steady and clear on into summer, with caddis flies and mayflies rising from it every evening, and the giant spruce and fir trees shadowing it, keeping it cool and alive. . . .

Small cycles radiated into larger ones. I kept following them — noticing different ones each day — and continue to. I became more comfortable moving through the woods — slipping between alder, climbing under and over the lattice-work of lodgepole blowdown, crossing streams on slippery cedar logs, climbing the rock cliffs, descending the avalanche chutes into the parklike stands of old-growth larch, their needles brilliant gold in the autumn, and brilliant gold underfoot, as if moving across a land padded with gold, and an inch of black soil atop the rocky rubble-traces of glaciers; sometimes two inches of soil, sometimes three, but then rock, with the soil so thin underfoot that you did not have to be a scientist to understand that one shot was all most of this place was ever going to have at grace — that it had taken some of these trees, these forests, five hundred years to achieve climax, five hundred years and three inches, and that once you swept them clean, the soil would go with them, and for a long time there would be only emptiness, rather than grace — that then there would be only the echo of grace.

I hiked around, just watching and listening. Making up my own mind. Noticing the differences between logged and unlogged areas. Not all logged areas had that confusion of spirit or loss of grace; some of them retained, or reshaped, the grace of the woods (or rather, the grace of the woods altered itself and still flowed around and through those areas that had been logged with care and respect).

But even those areas compared in no way with the untouched areas — the incredible vitality of cycles still ongoing in the deep places of the valley — the last untouched corners.

I realize that the point at which what was being done to the valley began to hurt me deeply was the time I first began to feel that I was starting to fit: that the landscape and I were engaged in a relationship. That I was being reshaped and refashioned, to better fit it in spirit and desire. That I was neither fighting this nor resisting it. As it became my home, the wounds that were being inflicted upon it — the insults — became my own.

No one can say for sure when a place becomes your home, or when a fit is achieved, or peace, any more than one can say when a river best fits the valley through which it cuts. It flows and changes, shifts — cuts deep in some places, fills in in others. It transports sediment, logs and lives. It makes music in the day and in the night. Animals come down out of the mountains at dusk to stand at the river's edge and drink. In the dimness, as light fails, the animals sometimes cross the river, wading or swimming.

Even the valley itself is moving — shifting slightly, the mountains like the slowest yet most powerful pistons in the world, some rising and others falling — the valley sinking and tilting toward the ocean — and as it sinks, it carries within it, as if in a bowl or a nest, all the surprises, secrets and cycles — all the miracles — anyone could ever ask for: more miracles than even the most uncompromising glutton could desire. We are all born with an appreciation of, a love and a need for beauty and grace.

But as if frightened of it, we carve, prod and poke at it. We view mystery as the enemy of knowledge, and in trying to find knowledge we end up attempting to harm the sheath of mystery which encases that knowledge — cutting or attacking that mystery, in either fear or anger — and in so doing, harming or altering the knowledge that lies beneath that mystery.

We take in a manner that does not replenish. We search out the last corners to do injury to them as if we have become confused — as if forgetting that we cannot live, cannot survive, without grace and magic.

What I was hungry for when we first wandered into the valley, early in the fall — snow flurries already sifting through the high country — was wood. I needed firewood by the ton — more wood, it felt like, than the most ravenous timber beast. I desired wood, dreamed of wood — we had none and needed cords and cords of it, to heat the hunting lodge where we'd be staying. We'd fallen in love with the valley around one o'clock in the afternoon, that first afternoon that we saw it, and by two-thirty we had been asked to caretake this massive old hunting lodge in the valley's center — there were no phones or electricity in it, and for heat the forty-room lodge — all the rooms were empty — had just two wood stoves. We never could keep the pipes from freezing.

Forty rooms. A room for each story we intended to tell; a room for each painting.

Our old raggedy Mississippi truck broke. Then my chain saw broke. For some now-unremembered reason, I still had the moving van in which we'd moved West, so we prowled the back roads, going from clearcut to clearcut, walking up into those steep savaged lands to pick up stove-sized pieces of wood, scraps and chips and residues. Sometimes, we'd drag whole trees out of the slash piles, where they had been bulldozed and abandoned — and we attempted to fill the moving van with these odds and ends — carrying whole logs down the steep muddy hills like crucifixes before shoving them into the maw of the van, like lunatic, lost tourists searching for some kind of authentic souvenir. Our big yellow top-heavy moving van swayed along the back roads, moving slowly through the autumn rains and mist. There is a certain undeniable raggedness of spirit — a newness, a roughness — to the place. It is not a place for anything slick and smooth. It is not a place filled with easy certainties.

After we got the moving van unloaded and swept out the wood chips and turned it in, I raced down to Mississippi and got my old Ford Falcon, which I knew was too old for the trip, but which was all I had. The radiator was clogged in some places and leaky in others, so I patched the leaks with duct tape and, as per the advice of a mechanic at a truck stop in Louisiana — such a long second journey home! — I bought a box of Tide laundry detergent and dumped it into the radiator. The mechanic had said that the detergent would slosh around in the hot waters of the radiator as if it were inside a washing machine, and would get all sudsy, which would cleanse the rust-clods; and that was in fact how it worked, and I made it back across the plains and up over the mountains a second time, driving days and nights without stopping: except that some of my duct tape patches began to leak, and soap bubbles then filtered through those leaks, so that a steady, wistful stream of bubbles trailed me the last several hundred miles. And that was how I rode back into the valley, the car looking like some renegade escapee from *The Lawrence Welk Show*.

I took the back seat out of the Falcon and used it in that manner as a mini-pickup. I got the saw fixed and was back in business, cruising those back roads in the low rider, muffler and frame sometimes dragging in the back, such was the weight of the wood. Our friend Nancy, who has an eye for the woods, says that that was when she first made the guess that we would stay — that we would find a fit with this place — when she saw us driving back and forth with a sedan stuffed full of firewood, sparks roostertailing behind us in the dusk, hurrying to get our wood in before winter. Before the world disappeared beneath snow, before Canada slipped down over us like an avalanche; like the curve of a breaking wave, a typhoon of snow.

Those first couple of years were days of heaven — wandering around taking from the grace of the woods, and just watching things and listening: not yet sensing or understanding that the wildness that nourished this place — and us — was slipping away.

Two years — maybe a little longer — of free grace. It was as though those days were days of harvest: art. Paintings and drawings stacked everywhere. And stories, too, all of them fiction — all of them trying to give something to the reader. (It was as if the stories came from the woods and flowed through me out to the reader, rather than the contrary, which I would later attempt, wherein I would try to take from the reader: reversing that electrical current in an effort to get the reader to give something, which would then pass through me and back out into the woods. The kind of charge-reversal that happens sometimes when lightning strikes a transformer and sends the power surging back in the direction from which it came — often frying the transformer. . . .)

Slowly fitting myself to the new cycles I was learning — deeper cycles, more subtle cycles. Fiction, nonfiction; literature, advocacy. Letters to friends, letters to Congress. Adjusting the mix of them gradually, and hopefully in concert with all the other rhythms around. Slowly waking up to the rudeness and quickness of what was going on around me — the carving away into the last corners of untouched country.

Sometimes panic would spike up deep within me — electrical charges of fear registering off the scale — and I would want to abandon all art and spend all my time in advocacy. I still believed in art, but art seemed utterly extravagant in the face of what was happening. If your home were burning, for instance, would you grab a bucket of water to pour on it, or would you step back and write a poem about it?

A great work of fiction can become a cornerstone in the literature of a place, and a cornerstone or foundation for all manners of ideas, such as the importance of wildness and wilderness, or concepts of grace, freedom, liberty. A great novel can reach thirty, fifty, even a hundred years into the future, across history, with such an idea, whereas a magazine article or newspaper editorial might have a shelf life of about two or three weeks.

And yet, what good does it do that great novel to extend so far into the future — forty years, say — if the place about which it was written vanished, oh, thirty-five, thirty-six, thirty-seven years ago?

Art is incredibly important to me — fiction, especially. But there are thousands of fiction writers in the world, and only one Yaak. It would certainly not cause the earth to pause on its axis if I never wrote another story again. I don't think there was ever any writer about whom that could not be said.

On the other hand, if a thing like the wilderness of Yaak were to be lost — I do believe that would cause a hesitation on the axis, an imbalance — a friction and an injury whose loss — like the cumulative effect of so many others which have already occurred — we would be hard-pressed to recover from. It's possible art could protect the last roadless areas of Yaak Valley. But I just don't think there's time for it.

*

Cycles and rhythms — an extravagance of cycles still operating in the Yaak's roadless areas, a wildness of cycles, still connected to one another and weaving together to make grace — still making order, every day and every season, out of disorder. This is of course what art does — takes characters' actions and emotions, in fiction, or colors and shapes, in painting, and weaves them to make order, as nature selects carbon and hydrogen to braid and weave the magic of life. And as order and logic become increasingly lost to our societies, I'm certain that these things — art, and the wilderness — are critical to stabilizing the troubling tilt, the world's uneasiness, that we can all feel with every nerve of our senses, but which we still cannot name.

The cycle of dying trees giving birth to living ones — we're all familiar with this, familiar with the necessity of rot, and diversity, in an ecosystem: the way that the richness, or tithing, of rot, and the flexibility, the suppleness, of diversity, guarantees that an ecosystem, or any other kind of system, will have a future. I like to walk — and sometimes crawl — through the jungle up here, examining the world on my hands and knees — watching the pistonlike rise and fall of individual trees — noticing the ways they block light from some places and funnel or focus light into other places — watching the way, when the weaker trees fall, that they sometimes help prop up and brace those around them. Other times the fallen trees crash all the way to the ground to become fern-beds, soil-mulch, lichen-pads. It's not a thing we can measure yet, but I like to imagine that each different tree, after it has fallen, gives off a different quality of rot — a diversity even in the manner in which nutrients are released to the soil. The slow rot of a giant larch having a taste to the soil, perhaps, of bread; the faster disintegration of ice-snapped saplings tasting like sugar, or honey. The forest *feasting* on its own diversity, with grace and mystery lying thick everywhere.

*

Like the manner in which nutrients are recycled through the forest, so too are the movements of the animals through it like a cycle, or a pulse — a rhythm of blood, chlorophyll and magic: especially the migratory patterns. There are a lot of deer in the valley — an overabundance, or sign of imbalance, some would say — against which, of course, a correction will always occur, as long as the earth corrects itself to the sun; for as long as there is gravity. It — the rhythm of the increasing deer herds — becomes more pronounced, more visible — more strongly felt — each winter.

In spring, summer and fall, the deer occupy nearly every square foot of the valley; it would be difficult for you to go anywhere here during those seasons where you could not find deer, or the signs of deer. But then as winter's snows cover most of their available forage, and as thermal regulation — south slopes, and heavy overstories and canopies — become critical, as temperatures drop, the places where the valley will allow deer to survive become extremely narrow. As the winter deepens, you can see almost all of the deer in the valley, and the elk too, being squeezed into a small fraction of the whole: the parameters tightening daily, so that each day, if you are deep into the rhythm of your place, you can feel the deer coming down off the mountains in the night, moving lower and lower into the valley and rotating toward those south slopes — crowding into spaces one-tenth, or one one-hundredth, of that which they previously occupied. You can feel the energy shifts, the lone deer and does with fawns combining and joining into huge herds, which then move like braids or ribbons, weaving their way along the same few ice trails, cutting paths deeper and deeper, browsing the limited winter food, and waiting for the release of spring. . . .

It becomes a pulse, winter like the contraction of a heart squeezing blood through the vessels of an organism — and you can feel the waiting for backwash, the waiting for the moment between beats, when the blood can wash back into the heart's chambers and take a brief rest — six months' worth —

before being constricted, squeezed tight again: the deer flowing up and then down the mountains, focusing and then spreading, concentrating then sprawling, and it too is like art, like breathing.

For so long, the story of the West has been that blood-scribing, that heartbeat of lighting out for "the territory" — the continental drift, westward toward freedom and liberty, as if some great magnetic store of it lies somewhere west of the Great Plains. But I sense that pulse may be — of necessity — finally changing and slowing, even reversing itself. I see more and more the human stories in the West becoming those not of passing through and drifting on, but of settling in and making a stand; and I think that there is a hunger for this kind of rhythm in towns, neighborhoods, and cities throughout the country — not just in rural areas, and not just in the West, but all over: that the blood-rhythms of wilderness which remain in us (as the old seas and oceans remain in us) are declaring, in response to the increasing instability of the outside forces that are working against us, the need for reconnection to rhythms that are stable and natural. And no matter whether those rhythms are found in a city, or in a garden, or in a relationship, or in the wilderness — it is the need and desire for them that we are recognizing and searching for, and I can feel it, the notion that settling-in and stand-making is the way to achieve or rediscover these rhythms. I can sense a turning-away from the idea, once pulsing in our own blood, that drifting or running is the answer, perhaps because the rhythms we need are becoming so hard to find, out in the fragmented worlds of both nature and man.

We can find these rhythms within ourselves.

I know we can all sense this blood turning; this incredible, increasing uncertainty in the world, and the instability of things — whether in the city or in the woods. What holds things together, and what tears them apart?

What is the value of art?

What is the value of a place?

Almost Like Hibernation

I LIVE IN THE WOODS. It's about as remote as you can get, in the Lower Forty-eight. There's no phone or electricity throughout much of this valley in northwestern Montana — the Yaak Valley. Much of it has been logged savagely — almost exclusively with large clearcuts — but there are still some dark coves, dark forests left. That's where we like to spend our time — my wife, Elizabeth, and I, and our daughters, Mary Katherine and Lowry. Mary Katherine was born four springs ago; Lowry, last spring. When it was time for Mary Katherine to be born, we drove down to the nearest town — Libby — an hour and a half away. We stopped on the summit leading out of the valley and took a picture of Elizabeth, with the snowy top of Flatiron Mountain behind her, because it would be the last day we would be able to take such a picture. Then we got back in the truck and drove slowly, carefully, to town.

It's different, up here. We live at the edge of the United States–Canada border and at the edge of the Idaho-Montana border as well. Animals from the Pacific Northwest overlap here and live together with those from the northern Rockies: wolves, grizzlies, woodland caribou, sturgeon and giant owls and eagles. Trees from both regions occur here — cedars, hemlock, spruce, fir, pine, aspen, ash, alder, tamarack. I spend great swaths of time mailing out cards and letters to members of Congress, asking them to protect this valley. It's almost all federal land, yet there's not a single acre of protected wilderness in the whole valley. Sometimes I mail out forty or fifty letters in a day.

We live in a tiny log cabin by the side of a pond. The pond is actually the oxbow of a river, formed by a beaver dam. There's just a single wood stove to heat the drafty one-bedroom cabin. It's the oldest cabin in the valley — built in 1903, when whites first drifted up here, looking for gold. They didn't find any, and drifted back south, out of this strange snowy valley of giant trees. The cabin has a large plate glass window that looks out at the pond. The pond comes to within twenty feet of the window. There's always something to see out that window. Blue herons stalk along the cattails, spearing with their bills frogs and small trout. The beaver brings her babies to the pond every spring. Bald eagles fly low across it, especially in winter — an extraordinarily beautiful sight, as they fly through the falling snow. The cow moose and her calf like to stand out there on hot days. Sometimes I take my canoe out on the pond and fish for a trout or two for supper, or else I catch them for fun and throw them back. In winter, otters play on the ice, and dive through holes in the ice, are gone for a minute, and then come back up with a fish, which they share with their whole family, not seeming to mind the twenty-below weather. One winter a deer fell through the ice, and I had to creep out and lasso her to help pull her out.

In the spring, when the geese and ducks come sailing in, their wings spread and feet dropped for landing, set on a long glide, it seems they are going to come sailing right on in through that big window. And in long summer twilight bats swarm the pond dipping insects from the water's surface.

It's a window to the world — or to the one we know and love. We used to live in cities, and then moved to small towns, but now finally I think we have found our level, somewhere way down near the bottom of things. About a hundred people live in this valley. A hundred people probably doesn't sound like a lot of people to someone who lives in a city of five or six million, but it seems like a lot of people to me. Think of what it would be like if you had them all over for dinner at once.

One family up here has a pig roast every Fourth of July, and we all gather at their place, but they've got a big yard. There are two churches and two bars in the valley. We play cards in the winter — pinochle — with each other, if the loneliness gets too bad. But it hardly ever does.

We're ecstatic, where we are. Solitude is a thing we crave. We're clumsy, in cities — when we get in a rush; when we find our hearts racing to make a deadline, to get to some place before the jam occurs. Mistakes get made.

But out here — it feels like we fit the cycles of things better. As if the world still makes sense — as if it is still intact, in places. It feels like less wear and tear, less heart-tattering adrenaline. Except for the paper struggle to try and protect the valley — to keep the last few uncut mountains up here uncut — I hardly ever get upset any more. I practice going slow, at a pace that can be sustained. I practice looking around at things.

You can see cycles in almost everything, out here. New things make sense and strange logic. We're learning things we never dreamed we'd learn — things we never dreamed we'd notice: the way snow covering a rotting log is the last to melt, which means it's well insulated, a good place for creatures to hibernate or stay warm; the way deer drop their fawns around the second week of June when the grass is lush and at its absolute highest, giving the fawns maximum concealment.

It feels like some weight of humanity has been lightened, if not actually jettisoned. No — definitely not jettisoned. Just put way out there, at arm's length. We don't get any radio stations — the mountain walls ringing the valley are too high — and there's no television reception, either. A few people, the two bars included, have satellite dishes that they can run off of gas generators, but we choose not to have one; if there's a football or basketball game we want to see, we'll drive the seven miles to the bar.

There's no telephone in our homes — just one pay phone

outside the mercantile, also seven miles away — the world's coldest pay phone, with a stump for a seat.

The only thing that really keeps us connected whatsoever to the world we left — the only thing, the invisible thread, thinner than spider's silk — is the mail.

I've made it sound pretty, and it *is* pretty — it's breathtaking, with a new sight every day — but in winter, even for those of us who love solitude, we're glad to see the mail. It's how we shop, how we speak, and how we listen to the outside world. And in winter, that which we have previously turned our back upon becomes once more appealing, even vital. Like sailors who would take along a supply of limes and other citrus fruits on a long ocean journey, the mail in winter becomes a thing that comes back into our lives, and which we want, once again: *human contact*. After going to so much trouble to distance ourselves from the bulk of it, it seems strange to now have this December-January-February hunger for contact: not a lot, but definitely some, and every day. Just a little; like a pinch of cinnamon, but without which the rest of the day would grow darker and colder.

The mail run comes only five days a week, Monday through Friday, around one in the afternoon; and in the winter, especially near the middle and end of it, that three-day stretch — from Friday's last mail till Monday's next haul — gets kind of long.

In the winter, you can hear the mail coming long before you can see the mail lady. There's something different in the stillness of the air: something that, having spurned, in spring and summer and on through the fall, we're now suddenly hungry for. Elizabeth stands on one side of the wood-stove warming her hands, and I stand on the other side. We look out the window, across the great field of white. Mary Katherine may be reading a book. She'll come to the window, too, and watch the mail lady take our letters-to-protect-the-wilderness, our Congress letters, out of the snow-covered mailbox, and slide new ones in. Some days we can barely see her through the thick-falling snow. Even the dogs sit up, sensing her approach: though they, too, do not venture far from the fireplace.

"Do you want to go get it, or shall I?" Elizabeth asks. We've got a set of binoculars by the window, and we'll watch and try to see just what the mail lady is putting in the box. If it's a fat mail day, we'll be anxious to go check it out. But if it looks like just a few thin circulars, I'll say, "Let it rot"; though we never do.

Always, there could be some small letter, or postcard — from Arizona, perhaps, or the Caribbean — tucked in among the hardware flyers that advertise snow chains.

We'll trudge down to the mailbox, wading through all that snow, pulling a bundled-up Mary Katherine on the sled behind us. One day's like the next. It's wonderful.

There's a thing in us that loves the winter, and a thing in us that is also made a bit uncomfortable by it. Even for hermits, there are limits. Still, we try to push those limits. We try to see how long we can go without having to go into town.

When we do go, the chores are dreadfully mundane, staggeringly predictable, each time: laundry, grocery store, gas station. A cup of coffee from the Hav-A-Java. Always, something from the hardware store. Sometimes, a haircut. Once in a while, a visit to the chiropractor. Elizabeth might swim; I'll take the girls to the park. The same slides, the same swings, over and over. Actually, I love it — that stability. And then the long drive home, to true security. If we can avoid town, we generally do.

You can get just about anything from a catalogue now, and in the winter, that's how we go about a lot of our shopping. It's luxurious, letting the goods come to us, rather than having to go out and get them. Skis, snowshoes, boot oil, gloves, sock liners, food, books — anything, everything. We've got a whole bookshelf of nothing but mail-order catalogues, like the reference books in a mechanic's garage.

When we need something, we sit on the couch and thumb through those well-worn catalogues, comparing prices and trying to gauge, from the photographs alone, just how durable the goods they advertise really are.

Once a choice is made, we have to decide how to get the merchandise delivered. The mail lady is petite, and carries neither chain saw nor ax. She drives a small red Subaru. If a tree splits from the cold or the wind and falls across the road, blocking her way from town to the valley, then no mail arrives that day, and the outside world stays silent. Occasionally, on days when she has not arrived by her usual time, I'll clear my throat and say, "I believe I'm going to run up to the mercantile for a cup of coffee" — and I'll check to make sure my saw's in the back of the truck, just in case I happen to come upon the mail lady, and just in case she needs my help.

Even more anticipatory than wondering if the mail will come that day is awaiting the arrival of the UPS Man. His deliveries are less frequent. He usually brings books, which we open ravenously. He's got a 250-mile route, and our cabin is the last stop. Sometimes he'll stand around in the falling snow and chat, in no great rush to start that long drive back across the snowy pass at dusk.

"I saw a mountain lion today," he might say, or, back when Mr. McIntire was still alive, "Today I delivered a package to the wagonmaster." (Most of the movie people live in other valleys, but we've always had the McIntires, since they came here over sixty years ago, just married. Mr. McIntire was, among other things, the wagonmaster on the 1960s television series *Wagon Train*.)

We stand there and talk, the UPS Man and I, as if to ward off the dusk, as if to hasten spring — and then he drives away, his big brown high-topped van swaying and slipping down the snow-crooked driveway, then disappearing into the falling snow.

The Federal Express Guy is the rarest of all sightings. But reliable: he carries a chain saw. He's a big strapping young man, with arms like some kind of melons; if his van gets stuck in a drift or a ditch, he simply wades out into the snow and lifts it free. He's got the kind of build that old fogeys like to believe they used to have, back in their glory days, and the Federal Express Guy is often overly cheerful, refusing to match the frequent glooms and silences of the landscape. He drives up in a rush, sliding to a fishtailing stop much too close to our parked trucks. He hops out as if he's got a bomb, or a live animal, in his envelope, and rushes across the snow like a commando.

But always, as with the others, he's welcome. And then he's off, in a rush.

In winter the woods are alternately motionless and then busy. We sit and watch, and wait, for glimpses — just glimpses — of the rest of the world's strange fury and speed. The mail is just the right arm's length. We sit, and wait, and move slowly, at our own pace, and at winter's. It's not quite like hibernation, but almost. Voices of friends, family and strangers come to us like whispers, in the mail, or like echoes. There's time to think about what's being said, and what to say back. There's time for everything — no rush — all the time in the world. It's a little frightening, and a little reassuring, both. It's why we're here.

The Land That
Congress Forgot

SOME ANTHROPOLOGISTS SAY that our species began in the homeland of the forest before venturing out into the grassland, while others say we rose up in the savannah, and that we were then driven into the forests for sanctuary. I don't really care which version is accurate, for I like where I am now, and it makes me feel right. It used to bother me that I loved the deep forest more than the sylvan meadows. I would acknowledge that there was some familiar longing, some sparkling blood affinity, whenever I came upon some small opening in the woods, some place of light — but still, I love the symphony and magic of the deep woods best, and for a while this seemed to suggest to me — if the savannah anthropologists were correct — that I was a misanthrope, turning back and away from the human race; that I was more ape than man, and that I had shaken off old human loyalties.

But the truth is the truth, and after a while it didn't matter.

It is dark here and rains a lot and the trees are big and there are mysterious assemblages of animals, groupings and relationships found nowhere else in the world. It is my home and I do not think any longer I will rush out into the bright meadow, lemming-like.

The Yaak Valley lies within Montana's northwestern boundaries like the corner of something — like the edge of all things, making the center of a new thing. If you were to fall asleep and then wake to find yourself in Yaak, unless you'd been there before, you would not recognize it as being anywhere you'd previously been.

The big jungle climbs and stretches over the tops of the low mountains. There are only a handful of peaks in the Yaak that push up above treeline. The highest peak is only about 7,500 feet tall; the river bottom is around 3,000 feet. Troy, the nearest town, possesses the lowest spot in the state, at 1,800 feet.

There's so much I don't know about this valley; but I'm learning: about the geology of it, about the plants and flowers, about the soil, and about how the black bears interact with the grizzlies up here, how the wolves and coyotes get along together, and the wolves and the lions. I've seen lions chasing coyotes off their deer kills; I've seen two bald eagles battling a golden eagle in mid-flight, with Mt. Henry's snowy crest in the background. It's a predator's showcase: I've seen wolverines and lynx, martens and fishers, weasels and owls. Everything eats something else, it seems, up here on the Canadian line, and I'm reminded of the old saying, "The closer you get to Canada, the more things'll eat your horse."

It's true that there is only a small double-digit population of grizzlies — ten? twenty? thirty? — and a single-digit population of passing-through wolves; and a dozen or so bull trout, down in Pipe Creek, beneath the huge clearcuts bladed out on the sixty-degree slopes of national forests, clearings that are now only memories of ancient cedars, and the soil and fungus of those old forests opened to blazing sunlight and aridity, and to the rains and their runoff. . . .

But those few wild individuals that remain in the Yaak are super-survivors, with genes that are critical to the future. They have survived the thousand miles of new roads built here since the 1970s, and the shuttling back and forth of their so-called roadless areas — having to abandon one sanctuary and move to a new, stranger one; almost always moving around, trying to make rhyme and reason out of those locked gates. Many of the larger animals — the bears and wolves — have come down into the Yaak from Canada's reservoir of wildness, and possess precisely the migratory abilities, the pathfinding urges, that will be required for our wild corridors to be linked back together in the West: for a genetic flow of health, of vigor and strength, to stretch as uninterrupted as possible once more from Canada to Mexico. I'm convinced that the Yaak is, and must continue to be, one of the corner-stones of this linkage — the most unique, atypical valley in the narrowest, most critical "bottleneck" of the northern Rockies.

There are places in the Yaak where I have seen elk, griz-zlies, bull moose, lions, grouse and coyotes all bedding and living in the same area. Everything lives together, here — everything is all crammed in on top of everything else. It's a small valley.

A lone woodland caribou drifts through the valley occa-sionally, doubtless following the old ghost scent of the herds of long-faded caribou who once lived here, but began to be pushed out earlier in this century. (The last verified sighting in Yaak was in 1987.) One year when I shot a spike elk, far back in one of the roadless areas (in the Yaak, the roadless areas average between ten and twenty thousand acres per core), I returned a few hours later with my backpack to find thirty-plus ravens, two golden eagles, and two coyotes feeding on my elk; the hide had been dragged off a hundred yards, with fresh bear scat leading me to it. . . .

It all comes together here: the rain lashes against the mountains, the forest types merge with one another — the Pacific Northwest mixing with the northern Rockies to make new and unique forms of diversity — and what comes from all this cataclysm is the deepest wildness.

Besides the traveling individuals that have survived in the Yaak, there are survivors that have learned how to hole up in the remaining core security areas; I've seen the largest trophy bull elk I've ever seen for four years in a row, bedding in the same spot. (Needless to say I've never been able to get up on him in hunting season). These last secure roadless areas in the Yaak are the perfect size for elk security — large enough to hold and protect them, but not so overwhelmingly large that they can't be hunted — but if these areas are whittled down any further, the elk will leave, though they will have no place else to go. . . .

Between 25 and 40 percent of the valley's grizzly population may be denning in one particular roadless area, and still the Forest Service is planning to build roads into this core, with a below-cost sales program whose purpose, I'm convinced, is to initiate long-term access into this last place.

Ah, but now politics is crashing into biology.

It's not just the animals who hole up and hide in the jungle. We do, too — the human residents. It can be a pretty rough existence for us, as well. There are those who trap, who tan hides, who try to log small green slip sales; those who build log and frame homes, who fix small engines, who hunt and garden, who teach, who guide hunters and fishermen, who write, who plant trees, who tend bar, who preach, who raise sled dogs and bird dogs. . . . Our livelihoods are as diverse as the animals', though one thing we have in common is that we all work for ourselves, not for big corporations, and that in itself is, I think, a form of wildness these days.

There are two bars — the Dirty Shame, and, across the road, by the river, the Yaak River Tavern. There's the mercantile, which sells gas and canned goods, and eggs, milk, and cheese. There's a volunteer ambulance barn, a two-room schoolhouse in the upper Yaak and a two-room school down in the lower Yaak, near the old mining camp of Sylvanite.

There's a fishing guide and a hunting guide. There's one cemetery, a small lumber mill — it burned, right before the fires of '94 — but the mill is being rebuilt. I have bought rough-cut lumber from the mill, and I love the feel and smell of it, love knowing that the wood I hold in my hands has come from the valley in which I live.

It's as much a place of indigenous peoples as we may have left in the Lower Forty-eight — a place of hunters and gatherers — mushrooms, venison, antlers, berries. It is a good land for craftspeople, a good place to take one's time with a single piece of wood, or with anything, rather than getting in a rush and making mistakes.

Because so many of us are hermits, or shy, or reclusive — because we simply live here for the solitude — engagement in political struggles is, for many, not a healthy choice. It's not why we're here. And often I feel as if, in working to protect the last roadless areas, I've allowed my private, healthy self — the one capable of great happiness and peace — to be lured into some place of turmoil, of never-rest.

But it is my home. There would be turmoil, also, if I didn't try.

Many of us who are working to protect the remaining wilderness of the Yaak understand the arguments, and the fears, on the other side. Never mind that if, say, every standing piece of merchantable timber in the 7,000-acre Grizzly Peak country were cut, it would only provide the mill in Libby with about two or three weeks of timber. Fears are as bad, or worse, than realities, and so in 1993, led by Steve Thompson of the Montana Wilderness Association and United States Representative Pat Williams (the sole Montana representative, due to the state's small population), we proposed the McIntire/Mt. Henry Conservation Reserve, in honor of two of the valley's early (1930) homesteaders — the actor and actress John and Jeannette Nolan McIntire.

The purpose of this area, which has been hammered hard by huge corporate clearcuts, would be to dedicate its use exclusively by sustainable, small-scale loggers, rather than continuing to let the international companies work it. They've had their chance, and have been harsh; now the proposal is for local small loggers to work it — horse loggers and roadside salvage sales, and selective timbering. Additionally, the remaining roadless core would be protected, and streamside repairs as well as reclaiming the lands scarred by roads would begin, in efforts to repair water quality.

This proposal was included in a Montana wilderness bill sponsored by Pat Williams the next year — he said that the

Yaak has "been hammered . . . in the past," and that he intended to "protect a small sliver of land between clearcuts."
Steve Thompson described the area as "one of the few wild
places in the Lower Forty-eight in which all of the original
pieces are intact: native old-growth forests, grizzly bears, bull
trout, mountain lions, cascading waterfalls, and even a newly
discovered fungus closely associated with the yew tree that
manufactures the cancer-fighting drug Taxol. In the last few
years, wolves have ventured back into the wild Yaak Valley
from Canada."

After being passed in the House with overwhelming bipar-
tisanship support, the bill then stalled and died in the Senate,
with neither of Montana's senators, Conrad Burns or Max
Baucus, supporting it.

Cary Hegreberg, vice president of the Montana Wood
Products Association, called the dedication of the proposed
small-logger area "unconscionable," according to the *Mis-
soulian,* and said it was a slap in the face of unemployed
millworkers.

And so it goes on, that battle with which those of us who
live here are so familiar.

I have so many stories to tell of the Yaak: things I've seen,
with hopes of more to come. Flowing elk herds in the backcountry. A great gray owl sitting on a snag in the deep woods,
seemingly the size of a man, watching me approach. Rivers
and creeks and waterfalls; grizzly prints in the snow on a ridge
one October, fresh tracks which measured almost thirteen
inches by seven inches. A trophy whitetail staring across a
ravine at me, deep in the backcountry, one snowy dusk. . . .

The Yaak is wilderness, and the Yaak, though atypical to
our state — atypical to the world — carries the spirit of Montana, the spirit of a place without borders: even if many of the
lands do have roads bounding them now, carving and cutting
into these last places.

The big timber companies, some of whom have already
abandoned the state, have successfully sold much of the public on the idea that environmentalists such as myself believe

that logging is bad, even evil. I don't have sixty or seventy thousand dollars lying around to donate to some senator, but I do have a pen and paper. I do have words that come out of my mouth, and against the power of their huge campaigns, I can say that I use wood, and love much about the culture of logging. I love the rip of a saw, the muscularity of it — the smell of wood, the sound and sight of wood. I love going into the Rosauers' parking lot down in Libby, sixty miles away, and seeing the guys in suspenders and hardhats, with the chainsaw oil and gas cans looped together in the back of their pickups, and a saw tool roped to the gas can. These to me are as much a part of the culture and a part of the wild as the lions and bears and wolves.

That is the truth, just as it is the truth that five-hundred-year-old larch trees are not needed for phone books and toilet paper — that tired argument; just as it is also true that jobs in timber would last longer if more work were done on the trees that are cut, and if they stayed here in the state instead of going to Asia.

You can't talk about the Yaak without talking about timber.

You can't talk about the Yaak without talking about wilderness, and the wild things.

Where is it all going to settle? What is going to be taken from us, and what is going to be left?

Who has the Yaak on their minds, and who has it in their hearts? Sometimes these two are not the same thing. To me it is a sacred place, and I am worried for it and troubled by its history, and worried for its future. It still belongs to us — that wildness, a kind of which we do not see much any more — but it is being lost to us quickly, it is being bought and sold by those who neither own nor know it.

Four Coyotes

Z-Mountain is the only nearby mountain that's not swarmed under by the rush of forest. Avalanches sweep the slopes clean each winter and keep trees from growing on it. It has a strange, humming power.

Robert and I climbed it one fall. Robert was talking about coyote luck. He'd been camping in Wyoming earlier in the fall and a light snow had fallen in the night, and in the morning he found tracks where a coyote had walked around his tent twice.

"Ringed by luck," Robert's friend, Terry, told him when she heard of the incident. "Coyote luck."

Robert was quiet, going up Z-Mountain. His father, a doctor, was due in for surgery in a week to have stomach cancer cut out: a big one. Robert and I climbed hard. Robert's knee was hurting but he kept on. We didn't say much to each other on the mountain.

The next day Robert went back to Mississippi. "Good luck," was all I had to say. And then a week later I got a letter from him.

"My coyote luck seems to be holding," he wrote. "When they went into my father's belly they came out with the whole tumor and a complete cure, which was a result no one had even mentioned as a possibility. My grandmother died peacefully the next day and we buried her on the Sunday the first cold weather came down to north Mississippi. After the service, I was standing in the little country cemetery outside

Shannon, looking at a moldering ruin of steel and wire mesh in one unkempt corner. A little old blue-haired lady, of which there were plenty on hand, came up and said, 'That's where we buried that circus feller that died here in '34. Nobody had any money to get him a stone, and we didn't know exactly who he was anyway, but he had that cage, so we just put that there. Bless his heart.'"

The first time I ever saw a coyote up on Z-Mountain, which is very high, was on my next trip. I was alone. It was hunting season and I had my elk call and I sat on the knife ridge of the mountain and was calling and bugling to a bull far down on the back side. It was dusk and too far and too late for me to go down into the next valley after him. I was just sitting on the top of the mountain calling to him, and feeling that ferocious wind. The elk's shrill squeals were echoing down the valley and my calls were being carried away by the wind. I am reminded now of how Native Americans never said the names of either the dead or their respected woods-mates. They would call the grizzly, for instance, "Grandfather" or "Beloved Uncle" or "Worthy Old Man."

For this same reason I will not speak the name of this mountain any more, nor will I tell about the fourth coyote in this story. Or maybe the fourth coyote is the one that is always absent. I think it is some combination of those two things: what is in us, and what is absent from us.

I was bugling and looking down the steep slope when the coyote answered. I gave another bugle and he trotted out of the woods, looking up at my ridge with great curiosity. I was all settled in among rock slabs, crouched and comfortably hidden. I called again and with a sly look all around, the coyote — small and pale gray, almost silver — licked his lips, as if in a cartoon, and came trotting out of the trees, up the slick rock through a dusk wind (my scent was rolling straight down the mountain, right at him, but still he had to come see) — and when he got to within forty yards of me he sat down on his haunches and howled.

I howled back, and then began to yip.

He answered and started toward me again — breaking off at right angles at times, as if wanting to leave, but then he'd reorient himself whenever I yipped and head straight back.

He came all the way up. He got spooked when he saw me, curled up and tiny, hidden there among the rocks — and he lifted a paw and danced away, but I made cow elk whining sounds, or human sounds of sadness, or perhaps even coyote whines — all sadness sounding the same — and though he turned to run away, he could not bring himself to leave.

Always, whenever I purred or whined, he slunk back in, making a rough circle around me — I shut my eyes and tried to feel a taste of his magic, and I could — and he was close enough to touch, staring straight at me as if disbelieving (and admiring) of my deceit — that there was another creature in the woods so full of it.

Here was a human curled up like an elk calf, acting crippled but possibly not, making sounds, alternately, like an elk and then a coyote.

Which was I? Elk, man, or coyote? He had to know.

This was his mountain.

It was windy and cold in that last magic hour of light before humans go home and the animals begin to come out, and I believe I had his trust. I could have reached out and tapped him on the shoulder with my rifle.

He sat looking at me with bright sharp green-yellow eyes and a half-crooked, superior smile — as if he were *laughing* at my crippled predicament. I sat looking back at him, making small whining sad sounds: things were passing between us at a zillion miles a second — electron stuff, New Age kookoo stuff, emotions and brain waves colliding in the five feet that separated us.

We were understanding, and communicating, as surely and clearly as two old friends writing letters to each other across the miles, as they have done for all of their lives. The coyote was laughing at me for being so many different things at once, and I was laughing at him for being so different and brave as to come sit next to me, a man; a man with a rifle.

It wasn't enough to just sit there with him and be equal, however; I had to go and do something dumb by trying to convert him to the language of misdirection, and abstractions. Or maybe I was just lonely.

I wanted to see if we could communicate in my language, not his.

"Hey, puppy," I said, and his eyes grew wide, and I felt those waves that had been passing between us fall to the ground and disappear into the soil. He skittered sideways, *floating* away with his tail like a banner in the wind, loping in that sideways trot back down the mountain, watching me with an emotion for which our language has no word.

"Hey puppy," I called out again, when he was forty yards off — two seconds later? — and he began to run faster.

I switched back to howls and yips. He sat down when he reached the treeline below and looked back at me one last time but then he turned and glided into the trees. It got dark quickly after that. I am certain that if I had not begun speaking in my own language something even stranger would have happened.

I had hoped to see him again the next time I went up the mountain but I never did. I did see ravens diving and playing tag — they came to investigate when they spotted me, spiraling over like kamikazes — but I never saw that coyote again, though I spent several dusks sitting in the same place, curled up like an elk calf and barking and yipping and howling, calling for him to come back.

TWO

The first coyote I ever saw in Yaak was the winter I moved into another man's ranch while that man was away. I was in the greenhouse, writing, and it was about twenty below. You could hear sounds from a long way off. You could walk on the deep frozen snow without punching through it. There were two horses in the pasture across the road. They belonged to a man in town who was keeping them on my landlord's pasture.

My back was turned to all of what happened. I was writing when I heard a truck come ice-crackling down the road and stop.

The truck door opened and then slammed shut, and two beats later, I heard the blast of a rifle shot. I thought someone was shooting at the greenhouse; I thought that maybe they didn't know anyone was inside, though smoke was surely curling from my chimney.

I ran out toward the road, where a big man in a heavy coat was tromping up the hill with his rifle, striding across what I already took to be *my property*, though I had been there only a month.

Between us lay a dead coyote, stretched out on the snow in his beautiful winter coat. We reached the ruffian at about the same time.

"That coyote was chasing the horses," the man said. He looked down at the coyote, whose eyes were shut. The horses stood across the road, pressed to the fence and watching us as if we had taken away their playmate.

It was important to the man, I think, that I understand. I was new to the valley and it was important to him that he educate me. But there was a beautiful coyote lying in the snow for no real reason.

"H" (the man who owned the ranch where I was staying), "wants me to shoot any coyotes I see on his land. He and I have shot coyotes before."

I did not want to judge the man but I could feel a judgment rising from the coyote as he lay on the frozen snow where an instant before he had been running hard and fast.

"Fur's worth a lot this year," the man said, bending down and lifting the limp animal up over his shoulder the way he might lift a sleeping child.

"He was chasing D___'s horses," the man said again, as he walked off with his prize.

The horses watched as the man put the coyote in the back of his truck and then, carefully, his gun in the rack. He drove off, waving at me through the window as he was leaving. He looked strangely hopeful.

I went back to my greenhouse — to H's greenhouse — and because there was an echo ringing through the woods, and through my mind, I just sat there and tried to read a book, gathering in rather than trying to create. Something felt absent from the valley. In that hard cold it would take at least a day before other things moved in to slowly fill that gaping spot.

I don't mean to judge. If I judge, I will be judged. My only aim up in this part of the world is to observe, and to feel; to be happy, and to be sad. But not to judge.

So I observed. And what has happened since that time is that D___ ran out of money and had to move far away — to California — and he took a job where he cannot see the mountains, much less be in them. H sold his ranch, and I moved on.

D___ sold his horses to a man in Chicago, before going off to California. They were good horses, but old. This was six years ago, and the horses are dead now.

It's like I'm the only one left. It's as if I narrowly escaped judgment, perhaps simply by having my back turned when the shooting began, and then by not bending down to touch the coyote as he lay in the snow (though I very much wanted to) — and by not defending him with words or argument — the language of deceit — but by merely standing there and defending him with my silence, and by observing.

By making sure I saw everything, since he could no longer see.

They should have let him keep chasing those horses, is what I want to say. But I will not say it: not out loud.

I'll just keep on looking, and watching, and seeing. It's like that's what he passed on to me — lying there in cold snow with his eyes shut. And then being carried away, over the man's shoulder — head and feet bobbing, as the man walked.

D___'s gone, H is gone, the horses are gone, but that coyote and I are still here.

I am not always in control when I go into the woods, and I do not care. I think there is a thing in me now that I did not come into the world with, but which I will be leaving with, and it feels good.

THREE

One spring morning I was out walking in the woods behind our cabin with my two beloved hounds, Homer and Ann. They were running ahead of me, chasing rabbits in the fruitless way that they do, having not yet figured out in the long years of chase that rabbits run in circles while hounds prefer to run head-on straight and forever, in tune with the wild thumping drive of their hearts.

My dogs have good noses and they tend to think of most of the woods behind the house as belonging to them, in that human way of love being ownership, and they scent out anything new and investigate it. Ann — peeing Ann — even scentmarks like a boy dog, does raised-leg urinations, scratches duff, the whole thing. And where Ann pees, I pee, because I want the coyotes to respect our space. I don't want any trouble with them. My dogs are at their mercy, and therefore I am at their mercy. We'd never had any trouble.

One spring morning I heard the dogs begin to yip the way they always did when they sighted and gave chase to a rabbit. Half-beagle and half black-and-tan, my pups have time bombs in their hot weedy Mississippi hearts, which cause them to levitate and give chase, and at such moments it's as if they're being carried away on flying carpets. Their yips this time, though, changed, and were mixed instantly with snarls and howls — the language of coyotes — and I could tell that there was a terrible fight going on.

Thrashing, I ran through the woods, leaping fallen logs and running through cedar and fir branches, running for my life. I couldn't hear anything as I ran, but I ran toward where I'd last heard the commotion. I called out, "Homer! Ann!" as loud as I could, as if trying to break up a schoolyard fight, though I knew that back in the woods I had no reason to expect that the mere sound of my voice could change things.

I came out on an old grown-over logging road — more of a trail, now — and turned and ran along that, still calling the dog's names. When I got to the end of that path, I almost collided with Homer and Ann as they came barreling around the corner, their little beagle legs churning, pumping as hard as they could — moving faster than I've ever seen them go, with an Oh-shit, I've-done-it-now look in their eyes. I was thrilled to see them, and crouched with arms outspread, picturing a welcome-home hug, but they blew right past me, and at that same moment two coyotes — the largest ones I've ever seen — came loping around the corner, running as easily as horses, almost *floating:* a deep red matched pair as big as wolves.

The coyotes halted when they saw me — twins — and stood there with frustration and hesitation showing on their intelligent faces. They were not twenty feet away.

Their *hearts* were still driving, telling them to continue the chase (were they defending their den? Had they been chasing the same rabbit Homer and Ann had bumped?) — but I could see the gears changing in their minds; one part of their body telling them to stop while the other part said, Keep on, Go right over him, Go right *through* him.

It was as if, stepping into the middle of their chase as I had, I wasn't a man: that all bets were off, and they could do as they pleased.

They stood in the center of the path, tall and long-legged — I believe that if they had stood up on their hind legs they would have been as tall as I am — and they moved their heads from side to side, trying to look past me to see where the dogs had gone, and then they looked at me, trying to figure out how I had gotten there, and why I was standing between them and where they wanted to go.

All this happened within a span of four, maybe five seconds — and still they lingered — and then, they seemed to understand that as I was apologizing for my dogs they should not attack them, or me for that matter, and so they turned and headed back up the mountain.

There had been a brief passage of time when their bodies were still in control, and not their minds, when I'd been sure that they were going to jump right over me.

They were twice as large as my dogs; they were wolf-sized and could have easily polished them off. But they had been merely *loping* — sending the dogs home. We had crossed a little too far over the line.

It is an honor to live in their woods. Each day, I try to behave accordingly.

The Fringe

THE SECRETS THAT COME IN from out of the
woods: the health that the grace of the woods has to offer a
community. You can't measure this health or this grace but
you can know it and feel it — as long as you are of a place and
alive in the world, you can feel whether a place — a town, a
home, a forest — still has this grace, or is lacking in it — has
forfeited it.

I think that art is one of the spillover effects, one of the
indicators of the richness of a place. You can't measure or
capture quantitatively that richness or health, but I think that
sometimes art — like a wolf or grizzly or caribou — can be
an indicator of the health and diversity of a place. I know that
great art can arise out of great turmoil — our innate impera-
tive to make order out of chaos — to make stories of order out
of elements of disorder — but I believe that great art can arise
out of great peace and security and stability, as well — that
powerful art can come from powerful emotions.

Art is a response to a time and a place — what might be
called an excess of emotions and, in the richest examples, a
diversity of emotions. It is not a numbing or diminishing of
the senses — it is not a homogenization of the world.

A place is healthy if it has cores of wildness in it.

The spirit — and the community — the human community — of Lincoln County, is still healthy, I believe, because
of the roadless cores, the sanctuaries, in the hills and mountains above the towns of Libby, Troy, Eureka and Yaak.

Art comes sliding down off the mountains, every night. Art follows the creeks and streams and rivers.

In the way that the bears are said to be able to live in two worlds — belonging to this world as well as to the spirit world, because of their disappearance underground for up to six months of each year — I believe that art, though immeasurable, lies somewhere between the world of science, facts and math, and the world of the spirit: that it can be a transition — as when a bear comes out of hibernation in April, or enters it, in October or November.

You can measure the diameter-breast-height of a tree; but you cannot measure the magic of a forest, or the effect a healthy, growing wild place has on your spirit.

One of the powers of art is that it travels back and forth between these two worlds.

Where art exists, the spirit of a place still exists.

Way upvalley there is an old woman who swims in the frigid Yaak River. I use the phrase "old woman" with nothing but the utmost respect. She doesn't live up there year round any more — only from about April to September — she leaves with the first snows, as the larch needles are still flying gold through the air — but she used to live up here year-round; she and her husband moved here over sixty years ago.

Her name is Jeannette Nolan McIntire. She and her husband, John, were artists right from the very beginning. She was born in San Francisco, and studied acting and opera; he was born in Hog Heaven, Montana — the next valley over — and studied, well, loving the woods.

They were actor and actress before television, before motion pictures. They were Shakespearean actors in New York and London, and then, still in their twenties, hooked up with Orson Welles in New York to produce the weekly radio show "The March of Time," which dramatized the week's news and attracted millions of listeners in the way that only art can — crossing the country democratically, diversely, without re-

gard to income, race, rural or urban settings — no limitations, no borders: only the artists' talents.

She and Mr. McIntire saved some money. He wanted to go
to Alaska, but it would have been tough to keep up their
careers. They settled on this valley, which, back in the 1930s
was, people said, just like Alaska, if not wilder. They bought a
big old homestead — the northernmost ranch in the valley
— and, between trips to Paris, Japan, London and New York,
settled in. They had two children — a son and a daughter —
who became, respectively, a musician and a photographer —
art — and for a long, long time they lived happily ever after.

She lives in the same cabin, still. Hides and pelts hang
from the walls. John rebuilt an old barn and turned it into the
polished log cabin that became their home. It smells deli-
ciously of woodsmoke and hand-tanned leather and fur, antlers and roasting venison; candle wax and flowers. She's one
of those rare and most comforting of things: a physically beautiful person whose graciousness nonetheless exceeds even her
beauty. *You like to be around her.* She is like the woods in that
manner.

Art was their world, right from the beginning. The sound of
the children playing the piano; the sound of the river outside;
the sound of geese returning in the spring — and heading
south, too, in the fall. Movies were being made by this time,
and over the years, they were in hundreds of them. Mr. McIntire was particularly fond of westerns.

Sometimes I think that art is like a wolf, traveling great
distances around the edges of its wide territory, and chasing and hunting down objects of its desire: a deer in the
deep snow. Traveling laterally, across the land, like thunder
rolling.

Other times I think art is like a grizzly, burrowing deep
into the earth, traveling vertically like lightning: mining the
underground soil, the emotions of magic — the unseen, the
unnameable. That art — or a bear — comes in contact with

things that have always been there from the very beginning: the magic and meaning and grace in the rocks and soil beneath our feet — the plan of life that is coded into those rocks, waiting to blossom.

Mrs. McIntire tells a story of how there was art buried even beneath the foundation of one of the old outbuildings on their property, when they first moved up here. There was a trapper's cabin next to their barn, built right after the turn of the century, and it had a little earthen basement. The trapper had used this basement for storage — a desk, a chair, and some wooden crates — and over the years, some of the dirt walls had crumbled in over these things. One day the McIntires were down there, *excavating*, and they opened those wooden crates and found that while the trapper had been living up there by himself through those long winters, he had been writing plays — reams and reams of plays.

"And they were beautiful," Mrs. McIntire says. "We sat there and read those plays, and thought about him living here so long ago, just writing these beautiful plays, and we just cried. . . ."

There was, in those days, a 100,000-acre wilderness at the edge of their property. That roadless area has been whittled down (in only the last twenty-five years) to 13,000 acres — and, of course, even that small core is threatened with further fragmentation: yet another planned road should cut that 13,000 acres in half. Mt. Henry — the tallest mountain in the valley, over 7,500 feet tall — rose snowy above their homestead, snowy above their consciousness. It guarded their dreams.

There was — and still is — a fire lookout tower up at the top of Mt. Henry. The McIntires were friends with the fire lookout rangers, and each spring when the ranger rode through with his packstring, ready to check in for his six months' duty on the mountain, he would stay overnight with the McIntires: his last touch of civilization before going into the wilderness — but boy, would they send him out in style.

Elk roasts, garden potatoes, a bit of wine and maybe more; opera music on the hand-cranked Victrola, and maybe a dramatic reading or two. . . .

Art overflowing from the bounty of life; the river running clear and cold and fast, right outside the door. Stars, and goose-music. . . .

In the morning, the ranger would ride up to the Mt. Henry lookout. He'd communicate with semaphores, or by cranking electrical charges into the magnetos that were attached to a single thin steel wire that ran down from his lookout, through the forest (buried beneath the duff, over the years), all the way to the next tower, maybe ten or twenty miles away. These steel cables (you can still occasionally come across part of one) ran through the woods like veins or nerves, and when the guy on one end turned the crank, a little bell would ring in the next lookout tower, so far away, and that ranger — say, on Lost Horse Mountain — would know that a fire was out there. The ranger on Lost Horse could then turn his crank and send the message scurrying down his steel line, through the soil, over to the lookout on Grizzly Peak, who could then send his to the ranger on Roderick, and so on.

They didn't just send messages of science from the mountaintops; the Mt. Henry lookout would send messages of magic down to the McIntire children each night — they'd signal goodnight to each other.

Each night, in the summer, the McIntires would go out onto their porch at the edge of their meadow, the edge of the river, and would look toward the top of that lonely, windy mountain. They'd see the lantern burning there — one tiny light at the top of the mountain — and would imagine the ranger reading, or writing letters. The children would light their own lantern, would hold it up for him to see theirs, and then would extinguish it.

And they'd watch, as up on the mountain the light in the lookout tower dimmed, then flickered, then disappeared, only to come back on again: once, twice, goodnight.

*

The business about the Montana Wilderness Association and Pat Williams proposing a McIntire/Mt. Henry Conservation Reserve, to recover the damaged areas, to protect the last (much reduced) interior core of roadlessness, and provide jobs exclusively for small-scale, local salvage logging — that idea, unlike the plays and all the other art, did not just rise up out of the soil like some crocus bulb. It was a thought-out and crafted response to an act of devastation and disorder.

In the 1970s, Congress was deciding which of the public wildlands should be protected as wilderness. The lands that they could decide upon, back then, were mostly rock and ice. A vast low-elevation sea of timber, such as that which surrounded the McIntires and Mt. Henry, really had no chance. But the McIntires tried. They flew back and forth to Washington, D.C., to testify to Senate subcommittees. They wrote letters, filed appeals — they gave it their all. But in the end (though it was not really the end, for still the fight continues), the Mt. Henry area was released for clearcuts and roads, and another wilderness area, farther south — with much less timber — received the designation instead.

The Forest Service and local mill wasted no time. Some dead spruce had been cut out of there in the past, and now there was a lot of dead lodgepole, but for the most part — some estimates say 60 percent of the time — the mills went after the big green live timber: massive clearcuts, leaving nothing behind. (Sometimes even the soil washed away. Subsequent lawsuits arguing that there had been extensive water quality damages were successful, of course, but too late — the damage was done.)

In a cruel taunt, designed, I believe, to mimic the giant letters "HOLLYWOOD" that stand in the hills above that town, the clearcuts on the mountain across from their homestead, clearcuts which are still bald a quarter-century later — visible from space — were shaped and carved into the mountain and the soil so that they appear to spell out the giant letters H and A and C. (A popular slogan aimed at stopping clearcuts was Don't hack the Yaak.) It seems that the timber industry, or the Forest Service — who should bear ultimate responsibility — ran out of room to carve out the last letter, a K.

What congressman — what congresswoman — will dare to step forward to heal and repair this kind of savagery and excess?

Healing. They were of a place, of a community, even if their opinions on grace and art and the forest didn't always match those of some of the townspeople — especially those who believed the liquidation of the forest could go on forever, and who were employed by J. Neils (later St. Regis, later Champion, later Stimson, as a succession of corporations cut and then fled town, downsizing at every opportunity).

They were of a place, more than the people who worked in the mill, more than the people who came and cut the trees, and certainly more than the various stockholders; and Mrs. McIntire is still of the place, more than any of us — more than all save a tiny handful of the sons and daughters of the original homesteaders, who still reside, here and there, in the Yaak.

One of Mrs. McIntire's favorite stories about Mr. McIntire involves some trouble he was having with a little tractor — a D-7, perhaps — that he sometimes used for skidding bug-killed lodgepole out of the woods. It seems that one winter it quit running — something was wrong with one of the parts, but he wasn't sure which part it was.

It was too cold to work on it outside, so he disassembled the whole motor, brought it inside, laid the parts all out on the floor by the stove, cleaned and examined each one, then put the engine back together again, there by the fire. He kept trying it, experimenting, replacing parts. It took him all winter, but by springtime he had the engine running again. He disassembled it one last time, took it back outside, reassembled it, and had it working once more.

She swims in the river daily at dawn, her morning constitutional: beautiful as ever. She tells stories of when she was young, and first in love. She tells stories of when she first loved this place, too, and what it was like, then.

My Grizzly Story

I USED TO BE A SCIENTIST — a geologist. I find myself thinking more and more about the turning-away-from, the divergence, where I left the trail of science and turned down the path of art. They're both about invisible or buried things, but in art you don't name them — you just chase them, then let them go.

For a long time I didn't recognize that I had turned down a new path: it all seemed the same. Brushy, remote, lush — mysterious and shifting — something new every day — and yet with some reassuring constancy, some background, bed-rock, unchanging basic-ness, always at depth, just beneath me and just beyond me. It was like being a child. Nothing was ever identical — every day, every observation, was new: and yet there was the security of constancy, of stability.

The world appeared that way to me — stable, secure, knowable — and I know in my heart that that is its true nature — for thirty-five years.

But now it is as if the trail has opened into a meadow, a small clearing — and as if I must go across that clearing; and I am hesitant to do so. Every cell in my body is fighting that change. Everything in me fears that on the other side of that clearing, when I pick back up on the trail, things will be dif-ferent; that they will be lesser. Less orderly — perhaps even chaotic.

Scientists like to say that nature is in constant decay, con-stant disorder, but that notion comes from the laboratories and the Petri-dish equations, and it is not what I see in the field.

Instead I see nature taking all the loose elements, the chaos of that disintegration, and weaving everything back into life. This is what art does as well — makes order out of chaos, makes two or more disparate elements alike — weaves back the unraveling around it — and so I am not surprised that for a long time I did not realize I'd branched off of one path and onto the other: did not even recognize the fork in the trail.

And I am not sure how far down the other path I have gone — only that it seems I have come to the first clearing, at which I am pausing, unnerved.

If I could do it again — if I could go back, if I had stayed on the other path — (and what chance or hidden urging leans one left or right; what pull of gravity or metronome within?) — I would like to perhaps have continued fooling with microscopes, filter titration, and seismology; I would have perhaps liked to have bushwhacked in even deeper, trying to figure out a way to quantify, to measure, things that are presently immeasurable.

Instead, I find myself trying to name them, and be in their company — rather than trying to tame and corner them, hem them in.

I think that art is wild, in this regard. Which is why I am chagrined, again, to be at this clearing — fooling with letters to Congress, to be believing in politics — to be counting and measuring, defending and explaining the woods, the wilderness: to be advocating for a voiceless thing.

I feel distracted from the hunt; and as if the headwind I've been leaping into, catching my prey's full scent, has suddenly spun, quartered away from me, so that I can smell nothing; and yet I also feel as if I need to pause and make a stand, pause and fight, if I am to survive — if I am to have any hope of surviving and going on, at a later date — to continue in art.

I feel as if there's too much change going on: not enough constancy.

Too much chaos. Too much for humans to make art or order of; though if we, like so much else, leave, then after we are gone, I know that nature will keep weaving, and that it will be beautiful, whether cast in fire or ice.

I was up on one of the mountains I'm fighting to protect, when I saw the tracks in the new snow. It was a miraculous week in October, one I mistakenly entered thinking would be a week like any other first week of October — aspens and larch, cottonwoods and ash trees stunned with gold, blue skies, and the huckleberry fields burnt red, blood red, and geese flying south, south, with the music of their leaving. . . .

So in that regard I knew the week would be miraculous, as it has been for me every year, every October, but I did not have any idea that it would be beyond that. I was already in love with these woods; I did not understand there could be a thing deeper than love.

The thing in our blood that makes us love beauty — and beauty's depth, beauty's electrical charge — who would even consider that such a thing can be measured?

At what point should we set down our microscopes and tape measures, with respect to the woods, and say, *All right, enough; this thing — nature — is larger than we can understand. We are only a part of it, at the tail end of it — nothing but a curious fat little comma, near the end of a very long sentence.*

I was carrying my shotgun. I was hiking up high, hoping to jump grouse. I had started down low, hoping for a shot at a ruffed grouse, and then, as if drawn by some call, I got it in my mind to begin moving up the mountain at the edge of the roadless area.

I started climbing the steep slope, through lush rotting cedars, through aspen and lodgepole — going up into spruce grouse habitat. But I didn't see any spruce grouse.

So I decided to go higher — to go to the top — to see if I could jump a big juicy blue grouse.

It had snowed the night before, I thought it would be fun to track the grouse in the new snow, if they were up there — to hunt the grouse as one might hunt a deer or an elk.

I worked my way to the top, through an absence of grouse. It was one of those days so beautiful that it did not matter. Even before I reached the top, I had all but forgotten about grouse.

I reached the ridge and looked over into the maw, the velvet green bowl of uncut valley on the other side — the largest roadless area in the valley. I don't think I can keep the roads out of it much longer, as either an artist or a scientist. I think as a general rule slow forces (like art, or continental drift) have more power than quick forces (like lightning or road building), but that the quick forces can cut more deeply.

Sometimes.

It was windy up there, and cold. Just looking at that modest sweep of green, that sanctuary, soothed something inside me, suffered and relaxed so many tensions stored up: as when you, or someone else, places their hands and fingertips over your face, covering your eyes, and then runs their fingertips slowly down and over your face, drawing out all the worry lines. That's what it felt like, over my heart, and I felt happiness.

If there were any other animals stirring — ravens drifting overhead, or ground squirrels scurrying — I didn't see them. I walked south on a game trail along the ridge, grouse entirely forgotten now, daydreaming instead about big mule deer, and about elk — and out of the corner of my eye, I noticed footprints in that new snow, fresh human footprints, I thought, and my mind went *Ah, shit — someone's been up here on snowshoes* — and there was that usual momentary loss and confusion I felt when I found I wasn't alone in the woods. The wildness left me like wind leaving a sail.

I was about to turn around and go back down the mountain the way I'd come, but then I wondered why someone would be up here on snowshoes, when there was only a couple of inches of snow on the ground.

I went over to the tracks and stood over them and froze. They were picturebook grizzly tracks, slabfooted, with the long claws — and so large that for a moment — as when you first awaken from a dream — I could not make sense of the size of them. I could tell they were grizzly, but the size of them shut down something in my mind.

The little twenty-gauge popgun, the iron stick with the cardboard shells in it, felt like a crooked twig in my hand. I felt as if I were suddenly filled with straw, and existed for no other purpose than to have the stuffing knocked out of me.

The tracks were glistening; the snow crushed and still watery from the heat of the bear's foot. I had moved him out just ahead of me, and by the casualness of the gait, he? (there were no cubs' prints) had not been in any kind of hurry.

I stood there a long time. In all my years in the valley, and all the thousands of miles hiked, I'd seen grizzlies twice — both times at close range — but this, the size of this, and the beauty of the location — up on this windy spine, up on my favorite mountain in the valley — *the size of the tracks* — moved me in a way I had not been moved before. I stood there and held onto the feeling of fear and joy mixed, almost hypnotized by the strength of the two emotions. I think that in loving this mountain so deeply, I had begun to view it, even if only subconsciously, as my mountain — up until this point. I knew where the elk bedded down, knew where the berries were best — where the moose lived, and the grouse, the coyotes.

I had to follow the tracks — had to see where they went: what that bear's habits were — even if only for a short distance.

I wanted to see the bear.

There could be no evolutionary advantage to such a longing. It had to lie in the realm of spillover; the magic, beyond what makes sense or logic, to our short-term goals. It had to be in the realm of art. I moved along the ridge carefully, head down, studying.

The Yaak is a valley of giants — of herons, bald eagles, golden eagles; white sturgeon below the falls, and twenty-five-pound bull trout; lions, wolves, grizzly and black bears, great gray owls, great horned owls, moose, elk — all these *big* animals — but seeing this grizzly would be like seeing an elephant in the woods. Because the dominant, wide-ranging, no-fearing ones are selected against, many of the giant creatures — like the country around them — are becoming smaller with each generation.

I moved carefully, slowly, through the lodgepole. My body told me to turn around and leave, as did my mind — but there was some other sense, some other thing, that drew me — that overrode those two imperatives. I felt it and trusted it and walked carefully down the trail, being careful not to step in the tracks, and feeling very fortunate, very lucky, to be on the same mountain with this bear, to be in virtually the same point in time and space with him. Walking just to the side, and behind, his footprints.

I felt something filling me, coming from the feet up, some kind of *juice*, some wildness, some elixir. I walked slowly, carefully — expecting to see the giant head and shoulders just ahead of me, at any second, looking back.

But there was nothing: nothing other than cold air, and winter coming. To my right — to the west — lay the beautiful uncut velvet of the roadless area — the wilderness. To my left, below and beyond me, lay the swaths of clearcuts. This was the edge, and it seemed very much to me that the giant grizzly was walking the edge of his territory, checking it out before he went back into the earth to sleep for five or six months. Checking things out — noting the new roads below, and the newly savaged hillsides — the patchwork of them drawing ever closer, and I imagined that it was a ritual he did, every year; and I hoped that his sleep was not as troubled as mine.

But there was no trouble in my soul, in my heart, that afternoon. There was only glory and wonder — only peace and awe.

There are places and moments where we must put away the yardsticks and rulers; and it is the artist's job to convince us of this, not the scientist's job to even attempt to prove it — often with the very use of those same rulers and yardsticks.

Do scientists dream of howling?

I know that they do.

The tracks disappeared as the bear walked out of the thin snow — as the new snow disappeared into the open sunlit places. I thought of his four-inch claws and of how the mild sun must feel on his thick coat.

When I couldn't follow after his tracks any more I felt again a burst of reverence, a mix of fear and euphoria. It was as if I'd made a small new discovery in science — as if one curious piece of data suddenly and gracefully connected with another. It was like writing a sentence that surprises and pleases you, one that carries you from all that has come before into new country. It was about anything but control.

I paused, wanting more. I pushed on in the direction I felt he had gone. But after a while the wild juice inside me, the fizz of it, waned. I was still out in open country; he must have disappeared within the sanctuary of cover. I sat down on a cold rock in the wind, tried to feel the sun on my face, rested for a long while, and thought about what I had seen. I didn't want to leave the mountain, as I had the sense one has when one is in the presence of a great man or woman, someone who's meant a lot to you, and whom you finally get to meet. You want to savor the moment and say the right thing, but also, especially if the day has been long and that person is old and tired, you don't want to be a stone, a thing that weighs them down, and so you quickly savor the encounter and are reassured, almost relieved, to see that yes, there is something special and different about him or her, some force, something indefinable — a thing you can see and hear and feel, taste and smell, but not know or name — and then you say good-bye and leave soon enough.

That was how I left the mountain — grateful, more than grateful, for having seen the tracks — and for the bear having heard me coming and having moved slowly away from me, rather than toward me. I knew it was very important not to overstay.

It was late in the day. There was still about an hour of strong sunlight left, but already the light was turning from yellow to copper. The burned-out, frost-bright berry fields on the hill below me looked as if they might have just had a bear pass through them.

There was movement on the hillside below me — twenty yards in front of and below me, beneath a lone fir tree. I tensed, then refocused. A bird's head blinked nervously above the bunchgrass; then another, and another. Three blue grouse, poised to flush. Wide-open country. It would be an easy shot once they flushed and sailed down the mountain — or a seemingly easy shot, which is always the hardest. Too much time to think, and analyze.

I stepped forward to flush them, but did not shoot: and one by one they flew away, fat and juicy and lucky. It was unthinkable to me to shoot a shotgun on this mountain with any grizzly, but especially that grizzly, on it. It would be like walking into a stranger's house, upon first meeting him or her — say, the friend of a friend — and blasting a hole through the ceiling in the living room. It just wasn't imaginable. The grouse set their wings and glided into the trees, far down-slope.

I once saw a small black bear on this mountain. I came within twenty feet of him as he sat upwind, looking around as if confused; and five or six years ago I saw a grizzly up here as well. Not as big as this one, it was standing on a log looking down at me as I picked berries. My dogs were with me, and one of the two dogs saw the bear about a hundred yards upslope.

Fortunately, it was the dog that minds best — Homer, not Ann. I whispered to Homer, whose hackles were raised, to leave it and come over to me. And Homer did. Then I called to Ann in a low voice, and she minded, because she did not see or smell the bear, and because Homer had not yet growled.

I took the dogs by their collars and went downslope, believing at any second the bear would charge. At the bottom of the hill, when I dared look back up, the bear was gone.

A giant bull elk burst from cover; he must have been bedded down not a hundred yards from where the bear had been feeding. For a moment, I'd thought it was another bear — a giant — and my heart and everything else in me stopped for a second, until I understood it was an elk.

At the time it had seemed to me to be only coincidence that brought the elk and grizzly so close together.

Five minutes further down the trail, the dogs and I had come upon a big cow moose. My initial sight of her chocolate-colored hump stopped my heart, and then she raised her head and stared at me in moose innocence. When I got to the truck I sat on the tailgate and ate every one of the berries I'd picked, half out of nervousness and half out of joy. . . .

But that grizzly story was not like this one. It was a fine one, but somehow different. I'd had my dogs with me, and I'd left. This time I was alone and following the bear. It may seem foolish, but it was the only time I've ever done that — followed one. It's the only time I've ever felt the urge to do that — almost like an invitation. I can't explain it: only that it was a true gut feeling. It's fine if I don't ever get one like that again.

I was standing there lamenting the missed opportunity, the lost grouse — a brace, at least — when I heard an elk bugling in the woods below and to my left — not far from the country I'd been in, had come up through. It was a wild autumnal sound — and I thought with some sadness of the fact that the high pitch of the elk's bugle had evolved out on the prairies, where elk had once lived, because high sounds travel farther there — but in the last hundred years the elk had been pushed into the mountains, and in the forested mountains their high squeals did not travel very far. It was almost like an empty piece of baggage they'd brought — deep, subsonic sounds traveled better in the woods — and I wondered how long it would be before that beautiful flute music was lost to the world.

As if changing, even as I listened, the bull, close below me, ended his challenge with a series of deep coughs and grunts. I'd been seeing this bull for several years; he was a trophy, and I'd hunted him, chased him in large circles through the forest, but I had never gotten a good shot at him, and knew somehow that I never would.

I was thinking about slipping down into those woods and seeing if I could sneak up close enough to get a look at him, when I heard the deep coughs and grunts of another bull answering him, moving in on him: or what I thought at first was another bull.

I wondered for a couple of seconds why the other bull wasn't answering with its own high bugle, why it was just coughing and grunting — a much deeper cough than I'd ever heard from an elk before — and I then felt the blood drain from my face and upper body as I realized that it was the giant bear — that that bear was hunting the giant elk — was trying to lure it in for a fight.

It was a sound from ten million years ago, a sound from the Pleistocene: a sound from the center of the earth. It took my blood to a place my blood had never been before — old memories, old fears, that did something to my blood, something massive.

It wasn't true *terror* that I felt. I don't know what it was. I didn't panic. But it took no huge leap of logic for me to intuit that if my *blood* was frightened, or even made uncomfortable, then maybe I should be, too — and I left, went down the hill, staying downwind of the sounds: and above me, the two giants kept calling, and I wondered how it would turn out, and whether the grizzly was serious about stalking the bull, or only playing, only curious, as I'd been, when I'd first considered trying to sneak in on the bull.

Later that year, after the bears were asleep, near the end of elk hunting season, I was up there again, and I saw the giant bull running through the trees below me, and was glad he escaped: and I wondered if he'd known, that day he'd been bugling and coughing, that he'd been calling to a grizzly and if he, like the grizzly, had just been messing around. It was impossible to know.

That had been October second, when I'd seen those snow-shoe-sized tracks. The next morning I worked hard in the office, knowing that later in the afternoon I would be going back out into the woods again, and hungry for grouse. It was a lovely cycle that I tried to fit myself into every October, to work hard through the morning and early afternoon, but then to end the day walking, bird hunting. I didn't need a lot — even two or three hours was enough, as long as I could do it every day — as long as I could count on the regularity, the stability of it. In this respect science is very much like art: you have to do it every day, to stay in the rhythm of it. To stay sharp. To stay strong. And yet: this is good only to a certain point. Beyond that point, the overflow, the excess — the part beyond our knowledge or abilities — almost always comes into play. Call it luck, or grace — the "surprise" discoveries, which have been so critical to science's advancement. . . . What is this magic overflow factor that the universe has been blessed with? Is the quantity of it constant? Is it diminishing? Is it our duty to safeguard those places where we sense it may be richest — where it might even originate?

The next day I went out to hunt grouse again and also do some scouting for the upcoming elk season. There was a big patch of country to the north of me that had not had roads built through it, though it was bordered and ringed by them. I parked along one of those gravel roads and started up into the woods. Right away I saw a ruffed grouse, but it was too young and would not flush; it only stood on a log and fanned its feathers at me. I tried to make it flush, but it only hopped and half-flew into a cedar jungle, so I had to let it go. I pushed on up the mountain, hoping for a wild flush from a mature bird.

An hour later, I was a couple of miles up the mountain, but I did not have plans for the top. I wanted to stay lower, looking for ruffed grouse, rather than blues.

The sun was orange over Buckhorn Ridge. I was working along a deer trail, noting old elk signs. The trail followed a shelf along the mountain, a southern exposure, with aspens above and below me. I was going to cross it and then go into some big cedars and follow those woods up the mountain just a little farther before turning back and heading home. It was the time of day, late in the afternoon, when you are most likely to see all sorts of animals, though because of the strong wind, I did not think I would see any. Sometimes the wind was in my face, but other times it quartered from upslope, from the north. The aspen leaves were beautiful, shading to bright yellow, and they rattled in that strong wind.

I came around a bend in the trail — the whole valley below me — and saw a golden bear walking slowly toward me, not forty yards away. Too close; too damn close. She was smallish — about twice my size — and her thick forelegs were chocolate brown, while all the rest of her fur was sun-struck blonde.

The wide face, the round ears, the hump over her shoulder — another grizzly, but coming *toward* me, unlike yesterday's, and averting her gaze — not making eye contact. Swinging her head and shoulders left and right of me, looking everywhere but *at* me. I was stupid enough to believe for a second that she did not know I was there. The wind ruffled her fur, blowing from behind me now, like a traitor, and in that cold instant I knew she knew.

One yearling cub appeared behind her, ten or fifteen yards back, looking exceedingly nervous, and then directly behind that one its twin, also looking troubled: not playing, as cubs do, but looking hesitant, looking uncertain.

We were all too damn close. The mother stopped about thirty yards away, the villainous wind gusting at my back — and she circled a quarter-turn and pretended to gaze out at the valley below.

She was so beautiful in the disappearing sunlight that seemed to paint her that gold color.

Her cubs came anxiously up the trail behind her — almost dancing in their nervousness, seeming to want to rise to their hind feet and turn away, and go back in the other direction, but obliged to follow — and I understood now that she too was nervous — that she was trying to move me out of her territory.

Instinctively, I circled a quarter-turn to the south and looked out at the valley, too. I dropped my head to show her I was not a threat. I felt fear, but even stronger, apology, even dismay. I felt incredible respect for her, too, and a surge of gratitude. We both studied the valley for a moment. I was waiting to see if she would charge — a thing passed between us, as if we were wired directly together, for a moment — the knowledge and understanding by both of us that she had every right, more than every right, to charge me (and whether in bluff or attack, no matter; she was almost *mandated* to charge) — and yet she chose not to.

I am convinced it was a conscious decision not to — that it was a thought, a rational decision — the mind overriding the body. It was merciful and generous.

There may be only a couple hundred grizzlies in the Lower Forty-eight outside of national parks (Glacier and Yellowstone) — and here were three of them, waiting for me to move aside, so they could continue down the trail, into history — into whatever fate awaited them.

I turned and walked weak-legged down the mountain in blue dusk, the sun now sending up orange sundial rays from its nest for the night, behind the far mountain. I reached the truck in dimness, half an hour later, and drove home to my wife and daughter. I held on to that new fresh feeling of still being alive for as long as I could; and even today, I can still feel, can still remember, the gratitude.

I am not going to speak against science. Science has its own wildness. But the science we have been taught pauses at the edge of borders, does not usually spill over, unless either by elaborate design, or by accident. We are taught not to leap.

In art, as in the wilderness, you can stumble into grace and luck, into magic, not just on the rare occasion, but every day; every single day.

I am too hungry, too gluttonous, to remain a scientist any longer. I want to consume — to devour — unmeasured things; to wallow in the rich overflow. To see it, or taste it, if not measure it.

A thing in my blood tells me that there are things in the world that, if touched and measured, disappear.

I do not mean to speak against science, or even to argue that we have too much of it. I mean only to suggest that we do not have enough art and wilderness. I think that magic is becoming rarer every day — rarer than timber, oil, or steel, and as a glutton, I want the rare things, the delicious things.

I want as much luck and grace as I can hold. Not measure, but hold.

Antlers

IT TOOK ONE HUNDRED and sixty thousand letters, it is estimated, to return wolves to Yellowstone and Idaho: to capture and transport wild wolves from Canada back into what remains of our own forests. Will it take two hundred thousand letters — or a quarter million, or a million — to protect the last roadless areas in the Yaak? How thrilled I would be if I knew that's all it would take; I would write each one of them myself, and be done with it.

But when the last roadless areas of Yaak are roaded, and clearcut — if that happens; if we allow the encroachment, the steady gnawing, to keep happening — where then will we get our wilderness, our old forests? Can you fit one on a helicopter as you can a wolf, and bring it in from Canada? Our ability to achieve the quick fix, purchasing a wolf or grizzly as if off the shelf, slapping a radio collar on it, and then turning it loose on our side of the border — those days are coming to a screeching stop. Right now, we're still in the mindset of being able to plug holes. But when the big wild forests are gone — when nothing but a hole remains — what will fill us, and where will we shop?

A day for cooking. I know I should be spending time in these pages chronicling the last days of the wild creatures, here at the edge of the century, in this land of giants — but it seems a day to pause.

Nearly everything is frozen — the snow continuing to pour down for the eighth day in a row — and there is a silence, a profound resting, all throughout the woods.

It is a time for death, too. This is the week, according to my journals, when, on walks through the woods, you begin to find more deer carcasses, the leavings of lions and coyotes, and of the winter itself — the absence of one thing, food, and of another thing, warmth.

This is the week, too, when the deer begin to lose their antlers — the antlers falling off and tumbling to the ground, first one side, so the deer is lopsided, but soon thereafter, the other, balancing back out. The trails the deer travel are packed down icy-smooth through the snow, and antlers line either sides of these trails like decorations in a rock garden, or like markers. In the summer after the snow is gone you can still come across these trails, the edges of them strewn with antler residue. The antlers will still be relatively untouched, except for having been gnawed upon by the squirrels and porcupines, who savor the phosphorous and calcium and other minerals held in the antlers.

The bucks no longer need their antlers for establishing and guarding their territory against other bucks, nor for establishing dominance. Survival is all that matters now — not procreation. The does have already been bred and are carrying the next season's life in them, and though the antlers might still be useful in defending against predators, flight is still the best defense a deer has. The extra energy used in carrying those antlers around is simply not worth it, so questionable is survival in winter: so fine the line, the balance of accounting between calories consumed and calories expended. So the bucks jettison their debt; the richness of the antlers, the extravagance of them, cannot be sustained.

It's possible, too, that the antlers are a liability in another way; it's possible that the predators know that in winter the male deer will be worn out from the rigors of the breeding season, and that that is another of the selective advantages of antler-shedding that has been sculpted into the deer, over the aeons. And doubtless there are other reasons as well which we will never know: but every year the trails are out there, lined with the casting-off of things — signposts of trouble in the present, but signals also of hope for a future.

There are times when I waver, when I think, *How foolish, how idealistic this is — a letter-writing campaign, like something one might do as a class project in the third grade. How totally inefficient, ineffective, in these days of corporate-owned politicians, and the corporations themselves so much more massive than ever.* The forest activist John Osborn has called money the "mother's milk" of western politics. (I don't understand why southern congressmen, in districts where trees are grown, indulge the massive subsidies made to the districts of western congressmen, where trees are liquidated and then the companies flee town; unless it is that the companies are so total now, so huge, that the timber companies have offices in both Georgia and Washington — in Arkansas as well as Oregon.) There are times when even the most idealistic among us must wonder, Are ideals even worth anything, any more?

Despite your knowing better, you begin to dream of the quick fix. Such dreams are born of winter-tiredness — a thing we must always hold at arm's length, no matter how bad things get — no matter if they get even worse, as current trends suggest may happen.

You tire of licking stamps and addressing envelopes — you tire of being voiceless. You notice that Boise Cascade, Plum Creek, Georgia Pacific, Potlatch, and Weyerhaeuser are active donors to the elected Congress; but then you notice that Microsoft is, too. What if the giants could be turned against one another? What if rather than continuously merging, they could be turned, like bulls with rings in their noses — or by idealism — to do good rather than such avaricious harm? What if Microsoft decided that the world needed a place like Yaak — not to visit so much as to just hold in one's mind? What if they, or someone as powerful — and their stockholders — decided that a thing did not have to be measurable to be valuable?

These dreams are dangerous. In the end, the answers always return to the gruntwork, to the rolling up of one's sleeves; the redoubling, or tripling, of one's efforts. If letters cannot change things, then we're screwed anyway, so you might as well believe in them, and keep pushing, keep believing — please keep believing. But on a winter day, staring out the window at six feet of snow with more coming down, you cannot help but let your mind wander, and dream of being rescued, rather than rescuing yourself. . . .

What is the value of the imagination? We probably won't really know until it's gone: until everything has been either decided for us or taken from us; until disorder and fragmentation completes its destruction of our social and judicial systems, mirroring our destruction of the woods. We probably won't fully know the value of imagination, spontaneity and creativeness until they are relics or artifacts from a more indulgent, excessive — richer — time.

The power of imagination is still rich in the Yaak. It is a force that is still intact in all of us. Whether in the pleasure, the anticipation, of looking forward to an evening's meal, or in the hand-to-hand wrestling of some great problem of the intellect — or in spiritual matters, or any matters — the tool of the imagination is still our greatest assct.

It is no coincidence that the more timber we clearcut, the poorer the communities around these clearcuts become; and that the more mines we dig, the poorer we get. The last of the money goes somewhere but never to us, and in the end we have nothing, have less than nothing, for our imagination has been taken, and we have only a memory of how rich the land once was.

Imagination — a kind of wildness in itself — used to be one of this country's greatest strengths: the ability to invent, and to question authority and the status quo — to ask *What if?* — to challenge, and ask *Why?*

No one asks Sony, or AT&T, or Plum Creek, or Amoco *Why?* We've had that power wrested from us — or have surrendered it. Some people think that it is the government's fault — democracy — while others think it is big business's fault. There seems to be a big difference between the two, despite their close affiliations, and we'd better make the right choice: not just for the sake of the woods and places like the Yaak, but for every other aspect that is relevant to our humanity.

Without question, a place like the Yaak — just knowing it is in the world, mostly, but also being able to wander into its deep cores — is vital to my imagination, as both an artist and a regular human being: as a father and husband, a citizen. Having access to peace makes me peaceful, and makes me want to be peaceful to those around me. One can only hope this is still contagious — that such connections can still be made, that those paths between us — what is called most frequently common ground — have not yet been fragmented.

And as an artist — a trade I used not to think was so terribly critical to the health of a culture, but which I am now convinced is at least as vital as any other trade — logger, geologist, preacher, teacher, senator, athlete, doctor — *diversity* — the depth of western wilderness has helped provide models for increasing the boundaries of my own imagination — that mysterious connection between body and mind.

I'm not saying you can't write a big story if you haven't ever walked across a big country. I'm just saying it makes it easier for me — and I know this is true for other artists I've spoken to — to imagine big stories, or big art (by which I mean that which is deeply felt) if one knows that there is a corresponding terrain of largeness of spirit — almost a boundlessness — still out there somewhere. Call it the unregulated wild.

If I can speak of the imagination, then I can speak of spirit. I must speak of the spirit of a place — again, one of this country's greatest blessings: an incredible diversity of *place*. What is a place worth?

Out of this country's braid, the United States' weave of

desert and forest, east and west, swamp and mountain, north and south, prairie and bayou, comes the fabric that we can all feel but can not measure or even name other than to say that it is American, and that we are Americans — not French, not Russians, not Chinese, but American. To be sure, Yaak is only one great strand — a thick rope — in the weave of these things — imagination and spirit — but these things are real and I do not enjoy watching them become weakened and even severed for the short-term profit of faceless shareholders for whom the words "place" and "rhythm" have no meaning; who scan each day's stock market quotations (whether they live in Beijing or Philadelphia) as if — get this — as if their lives, or their spirits, depended on it.

That's all fine and dandy, you may say, but you can't eat spirit.

No, you can't — but you can live longer and more fully on spirit than you can on clearcuts.

What is the spirit of a place? The writer and anthropologist Richard Nelson describes it best, I think: though again, for those whose lives are structured upon the short-term tricks of quarterly earnings or daily T-bond microfluctuations, he does not describe it in any way that can be measured or packaged, any more than one can quantify an act of kindness.

Nelson speaks of the seasonal comings and goings of life — the invisible trails left by the passages of the migrations of the animals — not just in Alaska, but all across the continent — as a pulse, a tracing, "a luminous sheath" of passages, emotions, and ways of being that conspires to wrap this country in its own unique spirit: the migration of cranes and geese overlapping paths and trails of the buffalo and caribou, the wanderings of wolves, and the waxing and waning of human cultures, human dreams and desires, across the land. No, you can't eat this — but neither can we survive without it — this spirit of place — and it is deep in danger.

*

All I want to do is read and eat, this winter day. Simple goals. When I go down into Libby for errands, on a day like today, friends will often ask what it's like up here: knowing that it will be snowing harder, and that the temperatures will be ten to twenty degrees colder.

We need that notion of an edge — a furthering of boundaries — in both our imaginations and the real world. I like to think that it gives balance to the communities of Libby and Troy — knowing that there is a roadlessness, a vastness, still beyond them. When I tell them that indeed the snows are deeper, that day — almost impassable — or that I saw a mountain lion run across the road — it seems to settle right with them; it seems almost to nourish.

I don't want to take anyone's job away. But I don't believe clearcutting the last wilderness will save or even create jobs; I think failing to protect it will cost us jobs, and more.

We are of a place: barely, we are still of a place, up here — the loggers and the woodland caribou, the owls and the elk. We are all hanging on up here and I hope we always will be.

This is the week the deer and elk lose their antlers — the week they line their trails with the evidence of their passings. My friends Tom and Nancy have taught their dog, Pagan, to retrieve any antlers she finds in the woods. She doesn't bring in every antler she happens across, but only those ones that appeal to her, for whatever reasons. Perhaps she actively selects those that she thinks will please Tom and Nancy the most.

It's quite a sight to see her trotting in from the snowy woods with one of those big antlers gripped in her teeth, her eyes bright with pleasure. You watch her enter the dark woods, and she's usually gone a long while: you wait, and the anticipation and pleasure build. You never know quite what the antler's going to look like; there are always a few long delicious moments of mystery as you wait for Pagan to come back from the woods.

Waterfall

SOME NIGHTS MY HEART pounds so hard in anger that in the morning when I wake up it is sore, as if it has been rubbing against my ribs — as if it has worn a place in them as smooth as the stones beneath a waterfall. Sometimes a calm, smooth, placid expression can harbor more fury than an angular, twisted one. And sometimes serenity can harbor more power than anger or even fury. I know that and I'm trying to get there — to peace, and its powers — but I just don't seem to be able to. The river keeps falling.

The sound of it, in my ears.

The Music and Harmony
of Large and Small Things

"I spend a considerable portion of my time observing
the habits of the wild animals, my brute neighbors. By their
various movements and migrations they fetch the year about
to me. Very significant are the flight of geese and the migration of suckers, etc., etc. But when I consider that the noble
animals have been exterminated here — the cougar, panther,
lynx, wolverine, wolf, bear, moose, deer, the beaver, the turkey — I cannot but feel as if I lived in a tamed, and, as it were,
emasculated country, would not the motions of those larger
and wilder animals have been more significant still? Is it not a
maimed and imperfect nature that I am conversant with? As if
I were to study a tribe of Indians that had lost all its warriors."
— Thoreau, March 1856 journal

LOOK WHAT I'VE DONE. Invited from my clearcut-rid-
dled home to read in Whitefish at a benefit for Vital Ground,
a nonprofit organization out of Hollywood that's trying to
raise dollars to purchase lands in the West that are critical
habitat for the beautiful glossy creatures that have been so
kind to Hollywood in the past — the grizzlies and the wolves
— I was perhaps unwise enough to make a scene. The reading had been advertised to the public as an evening of "bears,
wolves and writers" — implicit in the invitation and the fact
that donations were requested was the notion that it would be
an evening of fun and celebration, a day off from the never-

ending struggle to stitch the West, the American Rockies, back together. As luck would have it, I'm first up at the mike. They're trapped now, everyone in their seats, smiling and expecting poetry — literature — about the muscled hump of the grizzly and the night howl of the wolfpack.

Instead, I ambush them. Instead of giving them something — a nice reading — I ask for something. I read them a shrill diatribe about the Yaak, a small but vital cornerstone to the entire health of the West, and unfortunately a perfect example of the fragmentation that's going on all throughout the Rockies. I harangue my tender audience about the need to write letters to members of Congress so that they will designate the last few remaining roadless cores in the Yaak as wilderness. I hold up a copy of the ink-smudged mimeographs that will be on the table on their way out. Harsh facts are involved, I tell them. I tell them about the twelve hundred miles of logging road throughout the valley, and of the nobility of the animals that remain. I spell out the names of the senators and representative to write; I spell out the addresses. The members of the audience shift, squirm, yawn, roll their eyes and check their watches; they're aware already that the West is being fragmented.

But if we all know this, why is it happening?

One thing about a breach of etiquette is that it may leave you lonely at cocktail parties. Beware the zealot.

I know I've been behaving badly — passing out little Yaak-flyers at social gatherings, weddings and christenings included, at all occasions aside from funerals — but I can't help it. Time for the West is running out as it is being continually divided, and subdivided, while we sit complacent and idle.

An Indian tribe without its warriors, Thoreau said. The idea of wilderness needs no defense, it only needs more defenders, Ed Abbey said. All my life, my favorite animals have been those who could kill and eat me, Doug Peacock says. I see too much play in the Rockies these days, and not enough work.

We're losing the big animals first. In the Yaak, for instance, the animals that we most think of as defining the American wilderness, and the Rockies — the wolf, the grizzly, and other large animals ("megafauna") — are down to single- or double-digit populations.

The new information we're gathering about otters, white-footed mice and black-backed woodpeckers is vital, a sign of our maturation as students of the woods — but like some old-fashioned dinosaur who refuses to go into the age of computers, I still want to state the obvious, the oldest, most shopworn facts, for the zillionth time: that the American West — the Rockies — is still the only place in the Lower Forty-eight where we have wolves and grizzlies living together. Some of us have seen the statistics — that grizzlies are down to less than one percent of their former range, that wolves did not den outside of a natural park in the western United States for about sixty years.

The creatures that require less personal space than wolves and grizzlies can sometimes better adapt and move through, across or around our increasing fragmentation. But wolves, unlike salamanders and woodpeckers, will be shot by our own species whenever we see them. And certainly the grizzlies need the space that's being lost. In a way like no other creature in our country, grizzlies simply will not barter with humans. Conservation and ecosystem biologists refer to them as an "umbrella species" — meaning that, if grizzlies are present, everything else in that system will be present.

When it is raining, I want an umbrella, and believe me, it is pouring, and there aren't enough to go around. The spirit of the Rockies and its wildness is becoming tattered; it's falling apart.

Sorry if you were expecting something chipper.

The Forest Service, operating solely out of our billfolds, wallets and purses, has so far built for the corporate timber industry almost 500,000 miles of roads on our public lands. The four largest national parks in the Rockies — Yellowstone,

Rocky Mountain National Park, Glacier-Waterton, and Banff, up in Canada — are, without corridors of wilderness to connect them to one another, currently of no real or lasting importance to the health of the Rockies; they are like the large showy muscles of a bodybuilder who has ceased to work out. They're not going to last; the cardiovascular system's been ignored. The wild fresh blood can't get from one big muscle to the next. We must restore the body, for the Rockies to survive: for the Rockies to remain the Rockies, rather than a theme park. Pleistocene Park.

Maybe the spirits of things, such as wolves and grizzlies, in the Rockies, are meant to move great distances, or maybe they are not, but one and a half billion years ago, the earth that was residing not too far from my valley got up and left: was folded and pressed and thrust about seventy miles eastward, up over the Continental Divide and into what would much later become the Blackfeet Indians' sacred grounds, the Badger-Two Medicine region of northern Montana (which is also unprotected). The pattern, the rhythm, of movement — of big things traveling great distances — was set in motion by the earth itself.

And it only got stronger. With the new mountains in place, the frigid hearts of glaciers began to form up high, sliding up and down the mountains, cutting and shaping them for the species that existed then, and for the ones that would come later.

With sharp teeth the glaciers sculpted hideaway cirques, valleys, fast rivers, and then eased themselves groaning onto the plains, shedding moraine and clacking boulders and cobbles, stopping at the edge of what is now called the Front Range of the Rockies — where the mountains meet the plains.

There was a second glacier out on the plains, but there was also a narrow band of open ground between the two glaciers, a corridor running north and south along the Front Range. This dry land, free of ice, was a corridor for dinosaurs, and later for humans, bears, bison, mammoths, camels and ele-phants — big mammals, giant mammals, and their spirits, always moving across this portion of our earth.

Paleontologist Jack Horner has discovered fossils along the Front Range — zillions of fossils of a previously unknown dinosaur he calls a myosaur. Based on population densities (a volcanic eruption along the mountains pelted them with an acid rain of almost 700 degrees Fahrenheit), Horner believes the myosaurs traveled in great herds like our bison did. Once there were hundreds of thousands of individuals, even mil-lions, in those herds. But now, though the spirit of this im-perative lingers, our herds — elk and antelope — are smaller. They have few predators to concentrate them into the giant herds, and they have less country in which to travel. They are being forced to violate the big echo, the mandate, of the mountains: *be big and live big, dramatic lives. . . .*

Horner believes that Tyrannosaurus Rex followed these vast myosaur herds not as the arch-predator of all time, but as a scavenger. The myosaurs prospered when angiosperms — deciduous plants — came on the scene, which enabled the myosaurs to strip leaves, Horner proposes, and migrate north to south and back again, with Tyrannosaurus Rex, the terrible lizard king, weighing in at sixteen thousand pounds, plodding along behind them, feeding on the bodies of the drowned myosaurs at river crossings, the sick and the dis-eased, much as grizzlies move down low in spring to feed on green-up grasses and the carcasses of winter-killed deer, elk and moose. . . .

We need to sew the Rockies back together. Various en-vironmental organizations are undertaking a three-pronged program to try and help. The plan is to help protect (and, where possible, enlarge) the small handful of existing large cores of wilderness in the West. The plan is to work for the protection and recovery of the rare and endangered species still living in the Rockies. And the plan is to help reform the manner in which the commodity interests (fueled by our consumption) operate on public lands. We are all responsible, of course. It's all woven together. It's not so much a system of good guys and bad guys as it is a system of those who love the land failing to protect it.

Take the Red Desert of northwestern Wyoming. Most of the dangers of fragmentation involve one system being rendered useless within itself. But there used to be an elk herd that spent its winters in the Red Desert, and its summers in the Wind Rivers, a long way off. Now the Red Desert elk herd is cut off from the Wind Rivers due to logging and road building, and lives year-round in the desert, in total genetic isolation.

Sure, it's going to take a little work to sew these places back together. But are we going to do it, or are we going to just rollerblade off into the sunset?

I'm all for the small things. They stir my intellect with their intricate, almost incomprehensible beauties and complexities. But I am for the big things, too, the sight of which bypasses the intellect and shoots wild-juice and adrenaline straight into our hearts. The first time I saw a grizzly up here I was on a steep hill picking berries, when it stood and revealed itself to me. Despite having read for years *not to run*, I whirled and took two or three big steps down the mountain before my mind could kick in and say *Stop it.*

I love that.

"Save the grizzly! Save the sea otter! Save the whooping crane!" writes Doug Chadwick, who, having finished a beautiful and exhaustive book on the fate of the elephants, began to study beetles. "But what about the small, the slithery, and the leafy?" he asks. This, more than any jumble of technical jargon, any assemblage of word-proof and science-speak, describes the essence of what is called conservation biology, an ancient concept that American land managers (having ignored it for too long) are only now beginning to notice. ("Take care of the land organism as a whole," Aldo Leopold said to us a half century ago. "Nature will bear the closest inspection," Thoreau said almost one hundred and fifty years ago, "as if anticipating our coming trend to notice the big things but not the small — the other part of the whole. She invites us to lay our eye level with the smallest leaf, and take an insect view of its plan. She has no interstices; every part is full of life!")

Still, there is understandable reason why, in our panic, we've been practicing single-species conservation — what Chadwick calls "emergency-ward" biology. The big guys are the first to go. And if they go, it means of course that everything else will follow them. The essence and practice of conservation biology, beyond the recognition that all of nature is a weave, with all relationships interconnected, is that populations must not become fragmented, cut off from one another. If they do — if they are made into "islands" — then those populations will surely follow the course of any isolated population: they'll go extinct, swarmed under by the weeds of the world, unless there is recruitment of fresh genes. And the way that is done is through individuals. And the paths those individuals take are called "corridors."

In many respects the theory's so simple it hardly needs talking about. Areas of richest biological diversity are most important to conservation, because they're likely to have the highest concentration and complexity of relationships.

You protect the richest ecosystems first, and you especially protect those that are strategically located between other ecosystems, to allow genetic transfer between the systems.

Like some wild species hiding out in the dense, wet timber, right up on the border, I seem unable to leave, in my frantic heart, this one relatively small but cornerstone valley: the most biologically diverse ecosystem in the Rockies. If Yaak falls, then British Columbia's reservoir of wildness no longer has a straight shot down into the Salmon/Bitteroot County (from where it would have a straight shot into Yellowstone, to the southeast, or into Oregon's Blue Mountains, to the southwest).

Northwest Montana, and Yaak, similarly connects the

northern Continental Divide ecosystem — Glacier, Bob Marshall, Badger-Two Medicine, Swan Valley — to the Selkirks of northern Idaho, and to the North Cascades, which connect to the Central Cascades and the Pacific Coast Mountains.

If Yaak is not saved, if we allow it to fall, we might as well cut open the body of the Rockies and reach in and wrench out the bloody red heart and twist it free.

Because the Yaak so strategically links north to south and west to east, it has the combined, teeming diversity of all the ecosystems of the West. Not just bears, but nearly every other species imaginable: wolverines, woodland caribou, orchids, owls, sculpin.

Am I asking you to flock to this place to come see it? I am not: not until there is some system of preservation, some plan, in place. It frightens the hell out of me to be focusing on the Yaak — drawing attention to it. But it is so very much at the edge — so heavily fragmented, by the twelve hundred miles of roads, and the giant clearcuts — that if I do not draw attention to it, it will surely be lost. The lushness, the biodiversity, is still hanging on here. Even as I write these words, in the early fall, the chitter of a kingfisher is mixing with the *caws* of ravens. Earlier this morning, I heard coyotes; last night, I heard elk. There is still a symphony, still a harmony: barely.

A male grizzly may cover one thousand square miles in his life. (Leopold called this, with eloquent casualness, "cruising range.") Michael Soulé, known widely as the father of conservation biology, explains that "Roughly speaking, large animals are rarer — many orders of magnitude rarer — than small animals. Among mammals, there is a fairly consistent relationship. . . . The bigger the animal, the less its [population] density or the larger the home range. . . . Hence body size is a useful surrogate for abundance . . . and can be used in a preliminary ranking of corridor candidate species."

Once again, in the West, conservation biology always seems to circle back to the grizzlies. Never mind that once the great bear gathered in great numbers on California beaches to feast on the carcasses of washed-ashore whales, or that it roamed the deserts of Texas and Mexico, the prairies of Kansas and the forests of Minnesota. All we are talking about for right now is trying to hold on to what we've got. And if grizzlies don't have cores of pristine wildness — *they will not tolerate man* — and if they cannot move from core to core — then they're gone.

Soulé calls this phase "relaxation" — "the gradual loss of species from a habitat island," and adds, ominously, "Area-sensitive species, particularly the largest ones, are often the first to go." The big guys, he tells us, are keystone and indicator species, "strongly interacting with many other members of the community. . . . It may even make good sense to maintain such large animals in a system when expensive management interventions will be necessary to sustain them — for the disappearance of large animals often leads to the decline and extirpation of many smaller animals."

All of this is telling us what the heart already knows. The next words beyond "conservation biology," if that practice is not heeded, are the dreaded "restoration ecology" — a practice that will be as hard on taxpayers and wildlands as open-heart triple-bypass surgery is on a heart attack victim.

How much simpler, and cost-effective, to practice preventative medicine. Already, in the beleaguered Kootenai National Forest in Montana, costs are up due to the closing of some roads that should never have been built. We're paying to drill holes in the old roadbeds and to plant alders in order to speed recovery. The current Forest Service plan has divided the forest into numbered compartments, and when habitat-effectiveness rating for grizzlies falls below 70 percent (a mark I remember from school as being a D-minus), the Forest Service blithely assumes that the grizzlies will pack up and move into a nearby "displacement compartment" — some other place with a 70 percent rating — and they, the Forest Service, rotate these compartments every three years! It's self-deception at best, raw greed at worst. These compartments are sometimes called Grizzly Bear Habitat Management Units — GBHMU's — and remind me eerily of our government's similar shuttling of the Indians from reservation to reservation.

Grizzlies, like people, live in cultures, handing down behavioral information about their home — where to eat, when to travel, where to hibernate, where to hide — from generation to generation. Cubs typically stay with their mother for three years, so the Forest Service is essentially asking pregnant grizzlies to move, and even worse, is asking subadult bears, out on their own for the first time, to be able to seek out and adapt to these scattered-about, 70 percent–effective *displacement compartments.*

So many of the corridors between wild cores are not yet protected; they exist tenuously. One summer day I find myself sitting in a field up in the Yaak, barefooted with two local conservationists, Chip Clark and Jesse Sedler, and a third man, Evan Frost of the Greater Ecosystems Alliance, out of Bellingham, Washington. Evan has come here because he recognizes the vital location of Yaak — that it is the only logical corridor between the Rockies and the Northwest; and that it is on the ropes, that it won't last another ten years if we don't do something *now.*

We're talking about how absolutely critical it is to have corridors; we're discussing creeks in Yaak, elk wintering flats, grizzly denning areas, wolf runways. . . .

Like the trappers and mountain men who first came to this country almost two hundred years ago, we're describing routes and passes — special places that are a long journey away through wild, rugged country. Evan's listing the valleys to cross, the rivers to get from here to the Pacific Northwest. It's a short list, and you're there: fresh, new genes. Meanwhile, Jesse and I are diagramming how a wandering wolf could come out of Canada, down through Yaak, and head all the way to Mexico. *If.*

We're sitting there in the late-summer sun, surrounded by

cool dark trees. Clearcuts have scarred our valley, made it unattractive to humans, but there are still some cores left.

Evan and Chip and Jesse are spreading out mylar sheets to overlay on maps of the Yaak, computer generated maps that show remaining stands of old growth — *stability* — and grizzly radio-collar telemetry locations, and polygon mapping of elk herd movements. All this has been put together by Jesse in his spare time on a borrowed computer, data gotten from cruising the valley on his old motorcycle with a busted-out headlight, like Easy Rider, dodging deer in the dusk; and data gotten from Chip, too, during his and Jesse's stand examinations for the Forest Service.

People are going to shoot the big things, for as long as they're around, because, quite simply, people are afraid of big things. They assume that the big things are as full of the same kinds of hate and anger that our own species is, and so wherever there are roads into the wilderness, people all too often shoot and kill these big things when they see them.

The wolf that was killed in Yellowstone in 1994 — the first known wolf to make it back down to the park on its own in over sixty years — was DNA-tested and discovered to have come directly from Montana's Ninemile Valley — or, if not, then a direct relative of that pack's ancestry, which started out from Canada and Montana's Glacier/Pleasant Valley country, up in this dark wooded part of the state.

All through the Rockies, there is a clanging discordance resulting from our clumsy activities. It's a disruption of harmony and grace; it's a sound such as you might hear were you to drop a frozen turkey from an airplane onto a piano, disrupting the composer's performance. I can barely even talk about the woodland caribou. They used to be all through the upper part of this valley, but now we have only one lonely bull that wanders over every few years during breeding season, sniffing the ancient scent of the soil, old migration corridors, where once so many of his kind lived. (There are about twenty-five of them left over in the Idaho panhandle, about thirty miles away. . . .)

He's somewhat of an embarrassment the way he keeps hanging on (one year he showed up on the Bonners Ferry golf course). Neither the state nor the feds will list the woodland caribou as an endangered species in Montana, and I get the feeling they're all wishing he'd hurry up and die, and that the other two dozen would go ahead and kick off too, so that the problem would just go away. In several old barns throughout the northern Rockies, you can find caribou antlers and skulls mounted in the lofts, but they're old, almost as old, in some ways, as the dinosaurs.

Another species at the edge of extinction is the bull trout, a little-known fish still found in northwestern Montana. The bull trout doesn't run to the ocean, but it's just as vulnerable to fragmentation as if it did. They are definitely top of the line carnivores, as far as fish go, and by nature, by design, they are a migratory species, like just about every other big thing in the mountains. Bull trout live in deep lakes, but then travel up into the tributaries to spawn in the fall, sometimes traveling (when dams and fishermen will allow it) as far as 160 miles. They don't die after spawning, however; they return to their lake. Sometimes they live to be as old as ten years; perhaps in the past, say some biologists, they lived even longer.

They can get as large as twenty-five pounds. Though I've never seen one, I've sat on the banks of the North Fork of the Flathead in September and October, aspens and mountain ash ablaze with fluttering gold against a blue sky, and I've stared long and hard, watching for one of the twenty-pounders to go cruising slowly upstream, the sight of which in the shallow stretches of the river, on the way up into Canada, would be as improbable as that of a submarine. . . .

To keep from putting all their eggs in one basket, the bull trout have evolved so that some of them spawn every other year, while others spawn every third year, so that if there is a drought, or a fire, or some-such, a whole lake's population will not have been lost; there'll be some survivors back in camp who didn't make the journey that year.

There is a fine-tuned, ringing sound of quiet and almost inexplicable harmony up here; but you can barely hear it now, over the sound of the sawing, bulldozing, hacking. . . .

Once the bull trout have made their great cruise through the forest, beneath cool cedars and across shallows (their huge humped backs tingling with fear, perhaps, at the knowledge of ospreys and eagles above — traveling at night, perhaps, under the moon, past coyotes, lynx and lions) — once they've made it up to the creek's headwaters, the cool springs and gravel where they are to dig their redd and lay their eggs, they do so with a strength and passion that I someday hope to see. They bury their eggs a foot and a half deep, excavating (with their tails and blunt heads) a redd that is roughly the size of a pickup bed.

The eggs are fertilized; and then, beneath those gold larch trees, the red cliffside maples, and the aspen-blaze, with the days growing colder (higher oxygen content), the bull trout head back downstream, coasting, to their lake.

The fry are born around or on January first. They don't come out of the gravel after hatching; they wait until spring (225 days after conception) for that. But such is their fury, their lust to enter the system, the harmony, that even as immature fry they are predators; they'll roam around under the gravel and feed on anything unlucky enough to get in their way.

They remain in their river for one to three years, until they're about seven inches long, before beginning their migration down to the lake they can taste and smell and feel and hear: the lake they have never seen or been to, but which is their home, which has always been their home. These days there is an introduced species, lake trout, in those lakes, which eat the young native bull trout with a vengeance upon their arrival, but still the bull trout migrate, drawn by the music.

What's hurting them, beyond our introduction of lake

trout into the system? Roads, as ever; fragmentation. The dwindling of clean rivers. Sedimentation from road building, and from large clearcuts on the steep sides of mountains, so that the soil washes straight into the creeks and rivers, prevents the eggs from being fertilized. Even though the Yaak River is still clear, for example, there's about a quarter-inch of sediment covering the best spawning eddies. When I ask a biologist what can be done to save the giant trout, he tells me that "the answer loud and clear is habitat protection."

There are bull trout in the Yaak, the biologist says, "less than twenty of them" — but they're there. He won't let me use his name. He tells me the name of a creek and the first image that comes to mind is the scabrous lunar-gray clearcuts perched on, and sliding from, the steep slopes overlooking that creek. Less than twenty bull trout — maybe only ten or so each year — cut off by Libby Dam to the north, and by sedimentation downstream — moving back and forth through the autumns, as they have through the millennia — back and forth, back and forth, nature around them getting smaller and smaller in every eddy, in every deep pool.

"I've got this theory," I tell the biologist, "that even though the populations in Yaak are down to low numbers, they're maybe a hundred times more important, genetically, than populations that have higher densities. That for these individuals to have survived in the face of such heavy development, they must have supergenes, survivors' genes — and should be saved at all costs. I believe their genes can save the other populations."

I'm not a scientist any more, and I probably never was a very good one. Too dreamy. I respect scientists. But I feel like we use different languages sometimes, even when speaking about the same thing, so you can imagine my relief when the biologist says, "Exactly!" to my goofy survivor's theory. "The fish up in that creek are high-grade ore," he says. "As good as gold."

And hatcheries are no way to protect that highly evolved speciation, that lovely, ringing diversity.

"You can't reproduce the wild," he says, speaking my language. "There is no substitute for the wild."

The intricacy of the thing we're stumbling over, sawing to pieces, digging up and flooding, or draining; the harmony of what existed in the Rockies, before we got hold of the piano. The big things help us understand the small things. The big things are a gift to us, bequested to us from the foundation of all the small things below, the background and bedrock that lifts the big things up before us and sends them on their way through the mountains, so that an understanding of and appreciation for the wild will be visible to us even before our dull-lidded, quickly numbing gaze. . . .

Individuals; genes. The more numb we become, the louder nature seems to play, trying valiantly to get our attention — not to save itself, so much as to rescue *us.* That caribou down on the golf course in Bonners Ferry. The big things are trying to teach us intricacy, trying to show us, on the broadest possible scale, that we've messed up.

The wolf biologist Mike Jimenez tells of a lone male wolf he followed down in Idaho, the first known wolf in that state in a long damn time. Jimenez refers to that wolf as "a superindividual," one with those survivor's genes, as good as gold.

Hunting on his own, the wolf was bringing down adult moose, which was a thing I had not thought possible, and which I don't readily understand, when deer and elk were also available.

It's almost as if that wolf was trying to say something, trying to show something: and perhaps speaking not just to us, but to the spirit of the woods, the spirit of the bigness that is being lost.

The animals are not resting — the grizzly families being evacuated from GBHMU to GBHMU, and the lone wolves padding hundreds of miles at a time, from Canada to Yellowstone in a single year. . . . If they're not resting, why should we, who claim also to be bound up with them in the weave, take our rest? Any good work that is going to be done — any conservation biology that is to take place must happen now, this year, these next few years. We can rest only after we make a good resting spot.

"When despair for the world grows in me," Wendell Berry writes in his poem *The Peace of Wild Things,*

> and I wake in the night at the least sound
> in fear of what my life and my children's lives may be,
> I go and lie down where the wood drake
> rests in his beauty on the water, and the great heron feeds.
> I come into the peace of wild things
> who do not tax their lives with forethought
> of grief. I come into the presence of still water.
> And I feel above me the day-blind stars
> waiting with their light. For a time
> I rest in the grace of the world, and am free.

The white sturgeon, a river monster weighing up to one thousand pounds, is also found up here at the edge of my valley, in the Kootenai River.

I want to mention that sturgeon haven't reproduced in the wild in over twenty years — not since the Libby Dam went in (flooding the once-wild Ural Valley). I want to mention that all the sturgeon in the Kootenai are a population of ancient ones, with no juveniles, and that, like the one caribou, the dozen or more bull trout, and Yaak's handful of grizzlies, they aren't yet listed as endangered species. I want to tell how it is my dream to put on a scuba tank and mask and swim down the Kootenai River until I come upon one of the old giants, one of the thousand-pounders, as he or she rests on the bottom, its belly flat against the earth, feeling, perhaps, the last of those harmonics, the ones that mandate it to be big in this country, to be big or die, but not to compromise. . . .

How messed up is Yellowstone? One statistic says it better — or worse — than anything. Gold mines, clearcuts, irrigation projects, oil and gas leases, road building, livestock grazing, hydropower construction and that damn Imax-Zoo ring the park, preventing any sustained or substantial migration corridors into or out of the park; once more an island, a single loud discordant *clang* in what used to be a harmony. The biologist John Weaver lays this on us: that 67 percent of human-caused grizzly mortalities in the Greater Yellowstone ecosystem have occurred on 1 percent of the land — the private lands surrounding the park, choke-holding the park.

I hike up a steep timbered hill to a special spot I know of in the Yaak. It's at the edge of one of those roadless areas that we have to save, that we must start with, if any of this is going to work. It's springtime, and I've just read David Quammen's disturbing essay on the mysterious worldwide demise of amphibians, and how he proposed it may not be ultraviolet or global warming hijinks at all, but something more basic: habitat fragmentation, even at the level of amphibians. And it's never really occurred to me before, what frogs and salamanders do to maintain genetic viabilities, genetic vigor. A grizzly or a wolf can always get up and go, but how far, really, can a frog go, whether by flood (over the dam's spillway, or down the sedimented creek) or across the road? It's a whole new problem to brood about.

I am so much like the creatures in this endangered valley, and in all of the Rockies. All I want is a place to hole up and not be seen. It is late in the day, and I am in some old-growth cedars at about five thousand feet, when I hear the sound of frogs. I have been looking for bear sign, but Quammen's essay is on my mind, and I move quietly toward the sound.

I'm tired from hiking all day. I find the little pond from which they're calling. It's not even a pond so much as a rainwater puddle, a snowmelt catchment, about the size of someone's living room. I've been on this mountain a hundred times, but never knew it was here, ephemeral — and the frogs grow silent, even at my stealthy approach.

How long will this little high-elevation marsh last? In what brief period of springtime must the frogs find it, lay their eggs, and then hatch? And from that point, where do they go? What kind of frogs *are* these? I don't even know their damn name. They're not leopard frogs, or green frogs; they're kind of *funky*-looking, tiny, but with big heads, as if for shoveling, burying themselves.

All any wild thing wants is a place to settle in, a sanctuary — some guarantee of security — with the ability, the freedom, to roam if it wants to, or needs to. I take Berry's poem to heart; I curl up there on the hillside and rest, very still, waiting for the frogs to forget about me, and to start up again. I've heard frogs singing so loudly in the desert in southern Utah during breeding season — so many of them jammed into one waterhole — that the din, the roar of it, made me nauseous — but when this little chorus starts back up, it's nowhere near that thunderous. This pond's not that crowded.

Earlier in the afternoon, farther back into the roadless area, I'd heard a grizzly flipping boulders looking for ants; it was right up at snowline, and the boulders were immense. I feel certain it was a grizzly. There was no way I could go higher to see, though; I was afraid it might be a sow with cubs. I turned and went back down lower on the mountain without having seen it — having only heard, instead, the music of those boulders tumbling down the mountain. . . .

I lie in the spring grass like a child, listening to the frogs and thinking about the future: about grizzly music, wolf music, elk music and frog music. I try and feel the old earth stretching beneath me; whispering, or singing.

"I listen to a concert in which so many parts are wanting," Thoreau wrote, also in the springtime, in 1856. "Many of those animal migrations and other phenomena by which the Indians marked the season are no longer to be observed. . . . I take infinite pains to know all the phenomena of the spring, for instance, thinking that I have here the entire poem, and then, to my chagrin, I hear that it is but an imperfect copy that I possess and have read, that my ancestors have torn out many of the first leaves and grandest passages, and mutilated it in many places. I should not like to think that some demigod had come before me and picked out some of the best of the stars.

"I wish to know an entire heaven and an entire earth."

The music of predators and their prey: the kind of music we can hear most easily and clearly, though we are learning to hear the other, subtler harmonics, too, even as they grow fainter in the Rockies: the beetles and the rotting logs, the mosses and the frogs.

I'm still curled up as blue dusk comes sliding in. I'm on the side of the mountain that faces civilization. Two miles away, below me, there is a logging road: someone's been cutting firewood — I just heard his saw shut off. I imagine it's already dark down there. I picture the woodcutter, a neighbor, sitting on a stump and resting from his day's work: mopping his brow, and also listening — to the silence, at first, and then to the sound of the night.

After a while I hear his truck start up, and he drives away; I watch the yellow of his headlights wind far away down into the valley, to the river, as he heads home, where he will sleep, and rest, as will I.

We will not hear anything, as we sleep, but the frogs will keep singing, the elk will keep bugling and the wolves and coyotes will keep howling, until the fire within them goes out, and there is true silence.

Winter Coyotes

AT NIGHT IN WINTER I like the lonely, scary sound of coyotes. I like how it is after a day's work of sawing wood when light leaves and darkness comes, and the coyotes begin to speak.

It's a feeling like falling. Your sweat freezes. It gets colder once the sun is down.

All day long you've been big, sawing wood — or striding mountains — in the bright bold sunlight, and now you're falling. The trees seem taller; their reach extends almost to the stars. At such a time you may discover the true landscape, where you can project yourself only as far as your senses will carry you: a place where you apprehend the idea of size, and of what you are in the world.

The Blood Root of Art

LET'S DO THE NUMBERS.

In trying to sing the praises of a place, in fighting to earn or draw respect to an endangered place, you can only say pretty things about that place and think pretty thoughts for so long. At some point, you can no longer ignore the sheer brutalities of math, nor the necessity of activism. It's always a tough choice. You have to decide whether to use numbers or images: you have to decide whether the fight requires art or advocacy — and to try to have an awareness of where the one crosses over into the other.

I think it is like a rhythm — deciding when to choose the "soft" or supple approach of writing pretty about a place — writing out of celebration — versus writing about the despair of reality, the enumeration of loss.

The numbers are important, and yet they are not everything. For whatever reasons, images often strike us more powerfully, more deeply than numbers. We seem unable to hold the emotions aroused by numbers for nearly as long as those of images. We grow quickly numb to the facts and the math. Still, the numbers are always out there:

* Logging on the public lands in the Forest Service's Region One (the northern Rockies) cost the government between $100 million and $200 million more than they received for those sales in 1993; and,

* Siltation levels in streams are 750 times higher near logging roads than in undisturbed sites, often contributing to excessive erosion, flooding, scouring, road-slumping, and destroying water quality for sturgeon, trout and salmon, which — tough break! — have evolved to require clear, cool water. . . .

* *Forbes* notes that in the Gallatin National Forest — where recreation provides 16 jobs for every one logging job — the unemployment rate is 1.8 percent. Dr. Michael McGarrity writes, "The pristine environment, not logging, is the driving force in the current economic boom"; and,

* The Forest Service ranks as the world's largest road-building company in the world. Almost half a million miles of logging roads exist in this country — more miles than the federal interstate system — and another quarter million miles of logging roads are planned, paid for by taxpayers, for use by international timber companies; and,

* The Forest Service survey of 1993 showing 70 percent of Montana and Idaho residents oppose any further entrance to the last roadless areas in their states; and,

* Despite the influx of cheap Canadian timber — the results of the obscene forest liquidation going on up there, which rivals Brazil's deforestation rates — the timber companies working on public lands in the West continue to post record quarterly profits for their stockholders. By the end of 1994, despite a drop in timber prices, Plum Creek posted a record profit of $112 million; Georgia Pacific, based in Newt Gingrich's home state, had a 1,000 percent increase in profit. . . .

This nonsense about the last wilderness areas putting timber workers out of work, this big fat greed-suck lie about the last tiny wedge of remaining unroaded public lands being all that keeps sawyers and millworkers from reaching the eternal Big Rock Candy Mountain of secure futures and high finance — that myth (sold and packaged to workers by the timber products industry) runs counter to the *Washington Post*–compiled data that found that 80 percent of downsizing corporations neglect to pass on the savings to their workers in the forms of higher wages or more jobs. Instead, it all goes to the stock-holders — and 45 percent of those companies use the savings from downsizing to buy more labor-saving machinery, which then triggers a second round of layoffs within twelve months.

More numbers.

Not a single acre of the valley where I live — the Yaak Valley of northwestern Montana — is protected by our gov-ernment as wilderness for our future. It's the wildest place I've ever seen in the Lower Forty-eight. We all have special places that nourish our spirits, that ignite the sparks of our imagina-tions, that help make life more tolerable by sharpening the sacred edge that human lives can still hold. We all wonder daily how we should go about saving these places.

I'll go for long stretches at a time asking men and women and children to write letters to Congress and to the Clinton administration, as well as to the Forest Service, pleading the case of the unprotected Yaak, believing that if enough people write letters, the roadless areas that remain there — the wil-derness — can be saved; that an invisible thing like passion can hold a physical thing that is fragmenting.

But then, almost as if in response to some seasonal change, I'll succumb to the weariness of the activist — the brittleness, the humorlessness of the activist, the wearing down of one's passion and effectiveness — and I'll go for a long period (two or three months, sometimes) during which I believe that art helps achieve cultural change more effectively than does activism and the statistical rantings of fact. I'll believe that the bright primary colors as well as the pastel tones of art can carry more power than the black-and-white polarizations of activism. For a while, I'll think that *that's* the way to save a place — to write a pretty story about it, a pretty book — and so I'll change to fit that rhythm and belief, as if I'm in some cycle I do not understand but am nonetheless atten-tive to.

Later on in the year — for three or four months — I will then find myself trying to do both: art in the morning, and hard-core activism in the afternoons and evenings.

And then I'll wonder why my eyes drift crookedly; why I sometimes find myself staring at the sun, or why I feel off-balance.

Beginning in September, I disappear into the grace of hunting season for three months with my bird dogs. We chase grouse and pheasant; I hunt deer and elk, too, by myself, while the dogs stay home. It is like a submergence — like being in a cocoon or hibernation. I take from the land, in both meat and spirit — in what I believe is a sustainable manner — and I rest myself during that time for another year, another round in this fight to try and save the last parts of a place that has not yet been saved, in which and for which I am asking your help.

I don't mean to be insulting — traveling beyond my valley to ask your help. I know you have similar stories — identical stories — about places there: about every place that's loved.

What would you do?

How can the Yaak be saved — the last unprotected roadless areas in it?

I meant to use numbers throughout this essay — I had a bunch of them lined up, all of them perverse and horrible — but I got tired of them right away.

Writing — like the other arts — is not a hobby, but a way of living — a way, in the words of nature writing scholar Scott Slovic, of "being in the world." There is a rhythm that we must all find, in loving and fighting for a place — the integration of advocacy into your "other," peaceful life. I do not think it will always seem like a balanced or even pleasant rhythm. There will probably be long summer days of peace with only short stretches of darkness, in which you might be able to go a couple of weeks without panic and despair at the impending loss of the loved place — but there will also be long winters where advocacy and its inherent brittleness lasts for months at a time — times when the sun barely, if ever, gets above the horizon.

Even if you're not doing your art (or living your "other," peaceful life during this period), reading a great novel or viewing a great painting can be necessary solace during this dark time: and you continue your advocacy as intensely and passionately as you can, daring to take it all the way to the edge of brittleness — like a starving deer in winter. In the cycle, you begin, or your body begins, to create space within you for the return of art, or peace — order constructed out of disorder; a return to suppleness; sometimes you even warn, or mention to your fellow advocates, that you feel this internal space growing within you, and that because of it you may be stepping aside for a brief time; so that in this manner those just entering the crest of their advocacy cycle can help pick up the slack and continue forward as you rest (hopefully in peace) before you return to the advocacy at a later point, strengthened and invigorated. . . .

The writer, naturalist and activist Terry Tempest Williams is fond of the D. H. Lawrence quote "Blood knowledge. . . . Oh, what a catastrophe for man when he cut himself off from the rhythm of the year, from his unison with the sun and the earth. Oh, what a catastrophe, what a maiming of love when it was made a personal, merely personal feeling, taken away from the rising and setting of the sun, and cut off from the magical connection of the solstice and equinox. This is what is wrong with us. We are bleeding at the roots."

This is how I try to help protect the last roadless areas in the Yaak: with both brittleness and suppleness. It's been said that 10 percent of the world wants the world dammed, 10 percent wants it healthy, and the other 80 percent just doesn't care. I can rarely decide upon a fixed strategy — do I try and motivate further the 10 percent already committed to a healthy world, with brittle, angry urgings? Or do I try and coax the other 80 percent into the camp of the wild by writing as hard and as well — as pretty, as peacefully — as I can?

Again, it blurs. It becomes a weave, a braid, of rhythms; I do both, and I try and stay in touch with what Lawrence called "the blood root of things"; I try to make the right choices based on invisible feelings and rhythms, which are anchored in the realities of rock, trees, ice.

I think in large part the brittleness we feel when fighting — when advocating — for a place (versus the suppleness one feels when deep in art) comes from the almost totally dependent nature of the relationship: the relative lack of reciprocity. We receive far more nourishment from the grace of the woods, or the spirit of a place, than we are ever able to return. We can only learn to mimic the rhythms of the place we love — joining more tightly, in some small manner, in that larger weave before we extinguish ourselves: before brittleness wins out over suppleness.

Thomas Merton wrote of this fragmentation, this too-much brittleness, in one's passions for justice:

"There is a pervasive form of contemporary violence to which the idealist fighting for peace by nonviolent methods most easily succumbs: activism and overwork. The rush and pressure of modern life are a form, perhaps the most common form, of its innate violence.

"To allow one's self to be carried away by a multitude of conflicting concerns, to surrender to too many demands, to commit one's self to too many projects, to want to help everyone in everything is to succumb to violence. More than that, it is cooperation in violence. The frenzy of the activist neutralizes his work for peace. It destroys his own inner capacity for peace. It destroys the fruitfulness of his own work, because it kills the root of inner wisdom which makes work fruitful."

A little art can go a long way. This phenomenon is again a measure of the unevenness of the relationship between man's love-of-place and a place itself — the differential in that equation equaling, perhaps, the definition of grace. A love of place can fuel art, can fuel the imagination — can give nourishment to the supple, questioning, creative spirit in excess of whatever that place might receive back from the taker.

Art can be its own sort of advocacy for place; can advocacy — on the other hand — be art? Some say yes. I don't know. I'm not sure.

I had, once again, meant for this whole essay to be numbers: a landslide of numbers, like brittle talus. But I cannot tolerate them, at present. There is a space in me, this short winter day, that cries out for words.

I just read that when the freshman United States Representative from Idaho, Helen Chenoweth, addressed a Wise Use–Endangered Species Conference, she told the audience that the Yaak Valley was in northern Idaho, not northern Montana, and that it was so dead and sterile that there weren't even any bugs there.

I wish to differ with the representative. I live in this vanishing valley and it is still in Montana. Many of the logs from this valley, it is true, are trucked over to mills in Idaho (did you know that the recently developed single-grip tree fellers now require only two men to run them, whereas it used to take sixteen sawyers to fell a comparable number of trees?), but the Yaak is still in Montana.

Words.

Here is a list of some of the species still found in this place.

Bull trout, gray wolf, woodland caribou, grizzly bear, wolverine, lynx, fisher, harlequin duck, golden eagle, bald eagle, torrent sculpin, sturgeon, Coeur d'Alene salamander, great gray owl, Westslope cutthroat trout, flammulated owl, shorthead sculpin, northern goshawk, boreal owl, peregrine falcon, wavy moonwort, Mingan Island moonwort, Townsend's big-eared bat, small lady's slipper, common loon, sparrow's egg lady's slipper, kidney-leaved violet, maidenhair spleenwort, black-backed woodpecker, round-leaved orchid, green-keeled cottongrass, bog birch, crested shield-fern, Spalding's catchfly, linear-leaved sundew, northern golden-carpet, northern bog lemming, water howellia. . . .

There are more, of course — a Noah's ark of diversity in

this magical, totally unprotected wilderness — lions, moose, elk, bobcats, black bears, geese, grouse. The thing the earlier names all have in common is that they are on the threatened, endangered or sensitive species watch list: all imperiled, but still here, still hanging on — numbers be damned — as is my love for this place, and my hopes, in all seasons.

The Storekeeper

IT INTERESTS ME, the variations in flow and rhythm that conspire to make change. I used to picture the changes of seasons and events as the result of some incremental movement at earth's center: some perceptible straining against tension until the gearing of some cogwheel moved forward one click. And there are times when I still hold that opinion — the somewhat mechanized, simplified view, which makes it a little easier for us to believe things are under control. But more and more now I find myself wondering also if it — change — is more fluid than we can ever realize: that it is more fluid than even a river or the wind — that it is fluid *and* erratic, like some invisible animal that moves gracefully through the world for a while, then lies down to nap or rest, then gets up to feed and begins moving again — pacing and prowling through its home territory — its place.

I'm not sure when the harvest starts, up here; when the lightheartedness of summer ends and the hurry-up sweetness of autumn first begins to stir. We tend to hold these compartments in our minds, sectioning the months off into halves, the first and fifteenth of each month, and the seasons into quarters, like fruit, by solstice.

We had huge thunder and rainstorms last night, and today, the eleventh of August, did not in any way seem to me to be either a significant gear-tooth of change nor even have to it the feel of the motion of an animal or invisible thing getting up and moving from one place to another: but that is what happened.

I did my work in the morning, oblivious. It was a cold morning, after the front blew through, and damp and foggy; I had a fire in the woodstove at dawn, but still it seemed no different from the day before, or the day before. The coyotes had been crying all morning, even into midday, crying loud — so much so that I marked it down in my journal — but I had assumed it was for a reason that could be understood or explained or measured, and decided they had gotten drenched all night in the storms and had not been able to go hunting. It was an exotic sound, hearing them carry on in the middle of the day like that. I should have pondered it, should have paused and paid attention, but I just kept on working.

Later in the day I had to drive up to the pay phone to make some calls. The generator's been down for a month — no one can figure out why, not even the factory reps — and the backup is down, too, now. Because it's late summer, the solar panel's able to provide the energy we need; we pump water into the holding tanks on sunny days, and at night read by gas lantern, or flashlight. It's no big deal, really, but I was letting it get to me anyway. It was starting to bother me — going on into the second month of no one being able to fix it — and as I drove toward town, down the winding road through sun and shadow, and across the lazy river, my annoyance built, until that generator was pretty much all that was in my head.

I was already seated at the stump at the pay phone, punching in my first call, when Grandma Helen came up and gave me a hug and told me that Gail, the owner of the mercantile, had died that morning: she'd had a massive heart attack, seemingly from out of nowhere.

I put the phone down and said what everyone else had been saying, and would keep saying, through the day, slowly — "Unbelievable. I can't believe it."

She had smoked like a chimney, but hadn't been that old — fifty-eight. She still had all her energy and vigor; too much so, on some days, truth be told. If she didn't agree with something, she'd let you know real quick. She'd tell you how the cow ate cabbage.

Now I could feel it — the stillness over the town. The mercantile's the fulcrum of the valley: the place people come to hang out, to buy gas, to make calls; to rent a VCR movie in winter's stillness, or drink a beer, or to put a message on the bulletin board — the weight and birthdate of Sue Jantzen's or Lisa Mountain's baby, or the date of a bake sale, or anything — and Gail had been the one who had run this center-station. None of us up here like cities or crowds, but we liked the mercantile, and we liked and loved Gail. She, and the merc, was all of town we could take: the outer limits.

Now I knew why the coyotes had been singing and carrying on all day. I didn't know what they were saying, but I knew they knew.

Later in the afternoon I took my daughter, Mary Katherine, and my two hounds up the mountain to pick huckleberries. It was that time of year, suddenly upon us, as it always is: some shifting fault line or fracture between summer and fall. It's the first year she's been old enough to really enjoy and understand it, and after an initial period of eating every berry she picked — both of us stained purple — we settled into a bucket-filling rhythm. It was a little alarming to see how easily, how naturally, she fell into the pattern of acquisition, of hunting and gathering, laying in store for winter: how much it pleased her for the bucket to be filling. We *are* born with the capacity to look ahead, and plan for the future; I believe it is in us. I believe we do know how to look beyond the moment.

And so for most of the afternoon, crouched among waist-high bushes, we picked berries — picking the biggest, juiciest ones. The incredible simplicity of the act: the simple pleasure of the entranced rhythm — hunt, seek, gather; the simple, simple despair, say, at dropping a big berry, having picked one but then lost it in the transfer from bush to bucket, clumsy-handed.

The sun slipped lower, the late summer light grew softer, and that's all there was in the world, our soft, steady breathing, and the sound of berries going in the buckets, and the rustling of the dogs behind us, browsing the berries straight from the bush, their muzzles stained purple.

Driving home, we saw another young coyote, smoke-gray with a black tip for a tail, trotting boldly through a fresh-cut summer green hay field. The sunlight was lowering itself, turning into that brief kind of bronze lighting that happens for a while, late in the day, and yet the field itself was luminous and green, fresh from all the summer's rains. It's been a good lush year. Some of the hay had been cut, but there was an island of it in the center of the green field that had not been cut, which was tall and wind-waving — and when the coyote saw that we were watching it, it headed for that island of tall grass and disappeared into it, just disappeared.

We stopped off at the mailbox to check the mail. Nothing much: catalogues and flyers and such. I was thinking how if Gail had hung in there one more day — if she had lasted one more day (she hadn't even been sick!) she might have been able to see that coyote in the sun field, less than a mile from her store.

Turning onto our road, we saw a doe standing in the center of the road with a big spotted fawn nursing, tucked in under her hip. The fawn was really nursing hard, sometimes butting its mother with such force that it shifted the doe's hindquarters around at nearly a right angle, and the doe would shift and reposition herself, all the while watching us carefully. We had stopped the truck and were just watching, not wanting to disturb anything.

We watched them for almost twenty minutes. The fawn didn't dream there was a thing in the world beyond milk. And it seemed that the doe understood we would let the fawn finish: that we were in no hurry.

Finally the fawn looked up and saw us, and bolted, frightened, off into the woods. The doe flagged her tail and trotted off in the other direction. The fawn whirled, ran back across the road after its mother. We started the engine again and drove on home.

There was still some light left. There was something different in the air — Gail had alerted us all to it, but I could feel it now — and it reminded me that I needed to get the woodshed built, to keep the snow off the firewood. I had been thinking about it for a while, and had set out buckets to gather rainwater with which to mix the concrete, for when I would pour the pads, the pillars, which would hold the bottom course of logs up off the ground and keep them from rotting.

Mary Katherine and I went up into the woods and dug holes for the sonotubes — the shells or molds into which we would pour the concrete. We measured and spaced them, leveled them. She pretended to take measurements with the builder's square and the level and called out numbers to me in the dusk: "One, seven, thirteen, eight, one hundred."

We mixed the bags of concrete in the wheelbarrow, stirred them with the shovel, poured them into the tubes. Carved our initials into the wet cement, after smoothing it with a trowel. A light rain was beginning to fall — a mist, as dusk went into darkness. We could barely see, but I wanted to get them all done at once, to harden evenly. After a while it was past Mary Katherine's bedtime but we kept working, the way you sometimes do: not to meet any deadline, but because you are loving the work — if it can be called that. I kept asking Mary Katherine if she wanted to go inside but she said no, please no. We were damp from the rain but it was a warm rain and we were warm from working. By the time we were on the last pier she knew when the concrete was too rough and when it needed another shot of water. She would pour; I stirred.

She leaned in against my shoulder, watching me pour it down the tube, and she kept falling asleep standing up, leaning in against me. I carried her in when we were through and she woke up and changed into dry pajamas. I showered.

We got under the covers and I read to her, an old book about Theodore Turtle, as we do every night. It was a feeling like having gathered berries or firewood — having filled the day so full, full to the brim. It was still raining outside — a steady rain, now, and cooler, but warm inside. Mary Katherine was proud of how much help she'd been and was anxious to do more work tomorrow. She wanted to know what our chores would entail the next day.

I had already measured and cut and drilled the bottom course of logs. There was a pile of sawdust from where I had been working, so I told her that tomorrow we would pick up that sawdust, and maybe also, if there was time, climb a tree. I told her it would be another sunny day and that we might pick more berries, too. I went down the long list of things that needed doing before autumn, and in the autumn, all the things that needed to be gathered up, but she had already fallen asleep, after I'd told her about the sawdust and climbing a tree. She was smiling, and I know that those two things were more than enough.

Gail had had the store up for sale. She had said it was bad for her heart: the stress of running it.

I used to marvel at how many hours she put into it, just sitting there, waiting to provide us with whatever we needed, whatever we desired. She liked hunting season best, I think, when all the hunters came through, though she was fond of summer, too. It was a damn good day, and she had missed it, as we missed her — and the seasons kept moving on, and us in the world, as if riding on the back of something.

Cores

As shy as one of the dark-eyed owls, I never meant to get into it this deep. I never planned to shift my life from that of a self-sufficient hermit into one where, like some insatiable glutton, I was always asking for something: and never getting enough. And worse — never getting anything. Zero.

I'd seen such people, we all have — the soapboxers — and they were never attractive.

I should have been able to see it coming: my deep fall.

Running crookedly into the woods, hopping over logs and ascending some brushy slope, breathing hard, with tiger stripings of light filtering down through the canopy — I love to go into the woods — a ramble, an all-day hurling, out to some new place I've never been before, and back — sometimes getting lost, almost always getting lost. I should have seen how easy it would be to slide from a simple love for this valley into the full flame of obsession.

There is a new pseudo-science being touted by the Forest Service. They're conducting a big public relations campaign — always a bad sign — called Ecosystem Management (EM), which professes to be a new way of doing things — more selective cutting of the trees, for example, rather than clear-cutting them. EM will leave the superior trees standing, the Forest Service says, so that those trees' genetic vigor will be passed on. Strangely enough, there is no talk of the most basic tenet of conservation biology: the necessity of protecting wild, healthy, untouched cores of wilderness.

Such cores or anchor points can be viewed as reservoirs of health, which provide healing and nurturing to the surrounding places in a managed forest. Sadly, I have to conclude that EM is merely a ploy to gain access into these last roadless public lands — a way to let the fox into the henhouse. The Forest Service, under the directive of Congress, uses millions of taxpayers' dollars to build roads into these last wildlands, and then offers those forests' subsidized timber to the international timber companies. The Forest Service leverages money for this roadbuilding from the country's general revenue, but gets to keep a percentage of the gross profits — so the more timber that gets cut, the more Forest Service jobs that can be "created."

Big timber companies then pay off (in the form of PAC contributions) the senators they need, who in turn gridlock or obstruct the passage of any proposed wilderness bills.

And these senators then lean on the Forest Service to continue getting the high volume out — "getting the cut out," it is called.

I never meant to get into it this deep. I meant only to live in these quiet green woods and live a life of poetry — to take hikes, to read books, to lie in meadows with a bit of gold straw in my mouth and watch the clouds, and my life, go by.

Item: The Forest Service, required to provide Congress with a ten-year plan of operations every decade for the Kootenai National Forest, proposes in 1987 to cut 90 million board feet (most of it coming from the Yaak). The U.S. Fish & Wildlife Service biologists, with whom the Forest Service consulted, have determined that this is the maximum volume of forest that can be cut without harming the largest endangered species in the forest, the grizzly bear.

The timber companies wig out. A meeting is arranged between certain Republican senators, Forest Service officials and biologists.

The biologists change their opinion. They increase the cut by 50 percent, saying that they made a mistake.

Item: 1990. The chief of the Forest Service at that time, John Mumma, is forced to resign because he did not cut enough timber — because he refused, he says, to "violate the law."

And so we push on. Different Montana wilderness bills rise and fall; different congresspeople come and go. In the autumn of 1992, I was in Washington, D.C., judging stories and essays for the National Endowment for the Arts, a program that seemed by then perpetually under fire. My representative — now the sole representative for Montana due to our low population — Pat Williams, was fighting hard for reauthorization of the NEA program that had been so good to his state as well as to the country, the means by which artists, dancers and writers were brought in to teach and perform at meeting halls and rural schools. Pat Williams was battling Jesse Helms in the East, while back home, the Republicans were calling him Porno Pat.

I was big into letter writing by that time — I'd been pounding away for Yaak wilderness with dozens of letters each week, letters intended not only for the principals involved, but also for the most faraway and obscure persons as well. I sent letters to representatives from Guam, to the whole important seething mass of representatives from California — to all. I was hoping with this scattershot approach to blanket Congress with the odd name they would not forget, *Yaak*, so that when discussion came up of the public wildlands in Montana, even the most distanced participant could query one of the Montana delegation and say, "The Yaak is in Montana, right?" and feel that he or she was somewhat versed on the subject — and conversely, I believed in the power of the cumulative

effect that this could have: the accruing psychological awareness that every person in Washington knew that there was a
place called Yaak.

And if they knew it existed, then perhaps too they knew of
the scandal — knew of the specifics.

I was willing, and am, to work at it forever. To wear them
down, like the ocean against a granite jetty or a stone break-
front. I increased my mailing list hungrily; I didn't care how
much I spent on photocopying and postage. I would spend
everything I had. To do otherwise would be to let them — the
last wilderness-takers — proceed unfettered into and through
the valley. And then they would leave the county, with the
hills bare and the jobs gone.

In the autumn of 1992 I tried to improve my tightrope-
walking skills: the crossing back and forth between art and
activism. In the NEA sessions, I would read and discuss the
works of literature we had before us, and then on my free
time, on lunch breaks, I would hurry over to the Hill and
knock on doors. Some of the doors would open to me.

There are 435 members in the House of Representatives;
100 members in the Senate. First I went to Pat Williams's
office, carrying those rolled-up maps under my arm.

I dressed neatly, but beyond that — politically — I was a
slob. I'd called only the day before to make an appointment,
but had graciously been granted one.

It was a nice little office, warm and well-lit and well-used;
it had the feel to it of a busy newsroom. Files and files of
books and papers; papers spread across desks and such; all
kinds of activity.

The receptionist was friendly. She was from Montana.

I went back in the main workroom and got to talk with Art
Noonan, Williams's chief aide, first. Art pulled up a card-ta-
ble chair for me, and sat in one himself — a big overworked
cheery man, sleeves rolled up, black-coffee drinking, but still
bright and fresh, not yet burned out with idealism's failure —
all these things you could tell just from the air in the room, as
you can tell the condition of a forest when you are walking

through it — and Artie and I spoke for about half an hour. He talked a lot about his home town of Butte, and how it was recovering, after having been devastated by the exodus of mining interests after they'd taken everything there was to take. He talked about how government had been able to help the town to recover, phoenix-like, from that depression. He wasn't talking about wilderness — he was talking about communities — and we never did get to talk about Yaak, but that was all right, because I enjoyed listening to him. After a while the receptionist peered around the corner and said that Pat could see me now.

In the end all we can ever rely on, at base, are our instincts, our gut impressions. And the one I got from seeing Pat Williams (I'd met him once before, in Libby) was that he was honest and strong. I liked his handshake. His sleeves were rolled up, and he looked tired. I liked him.

I wasn't there to like him, though. The bears and wolves had sent me to this office. I was speaking for them. After placing the maps on the coffee table I sat in the armchair while Art stood near the doorway, listening, and Pat walked over to the window in a manner that the unfeeling cynic might have accused as being dramatic or practiced, but which I accepted as honest.

"This town," he said. "Every year, I wonder why I come back." He gestured to the gray sky, the concrete out his window. "Look at it. It's not home, is it? God, it's no place for a family. You come in wanting to do all this good, and you see what's necessary to get it done, and you see good people get trampled, and bad people, really bad people, ascend. . . ."

I sat quietly and listened. Again, it could have been just show — a cynic could have accused him of faking the emotion that he pretended to let spill out of him — of being an actor — but that was not the feeling I got.

Williams turned quickly away from his problems and asked, "Do the wolves use these wilderness areas, Rick?" He seemed so keenly interested in my answer that I thought it was a test of sorts, a way of gauging my honesty — and I told him what I would have told him anyway, the truth, which was yes and no. The wolves use wilderness areas because there aren't as many people there to shoot them. But the country the wolves would probably prefer if they had their choice is the land along the river bottoms where the towns are — because that's where the deer go in winter — to the lowlands.

Pat sat right down to look at the maps. We went over each roadless area briefly, and I described them to him. He knew their names, knew where they were on the map, and after I had shown them all to him, and demonstrated how only a few hundred acres would be taken out of the timber base, he pointed to the places on the map that he said he thought he "could do something for."

It was late in the day. We shook hands again and he said he'd see what he could do: and as later results were to prove, this wasn't the usual dismissive bullshit you hear now and then in life.

As I was leaving, I added one thing: I told him about the actor and actress who'd homesteaded up in the Yaak sixty years ago — Mr. and Mrs. McIntire — and about how the proposed wilderness above their homestead had been given away in a political trade. I told him how the Forest Service hacked the land around her homestead — the giant letters H-A-C formed by the clearcuts — in retaliation for her and her husband's nerve to stand up and fight. I asked if there was something he could do to acknowledge that wrong — if he could put their name on something up there.

He said that he could. He gave me his word on it.

It's weird, how a thing sucks you in. We're used to breaking things up into chapters — into labeling periods of our lives, and periods of history, as separate units, with sharp beginnings and ends. And looking back, maybe that's how I saw things at that time. But now it seems as though I had stepped into a lake: and had been ankle-deep in it for a long time, and then knee-deep, and then thigh-deep. For a long while I was in it up to my waist, though everything still seemed all right; I could fight the grass fires of Yaak with one hand, and write fiction with the other.

But the water level rose to my chest, and it was cold; it rose to my shoulders, to my neck, and by then it was getting dark, too. And then I was swimming by starlight, breast-stroking, both hands completely wet, all of me wet. The moon came up over the mountains and I kept swimming and am still swimming and cannot see the shore, but neither can I let them, Congress and big business, get away with what is happening in the Yaak, and elsewhere in the West: the war on the West.

Twelve hundred miles of logging roads in my wet green valley! Nearly five hundred thousand miles of logging roads in the United States, built by taxpayers, for the timber companies — eight times the length of the entire United States interstate system! These numbers make me want to run deeper into the woods. Numbers cannot measure what is being lost.

I do not wish to know a subdued Heaven and Earth, Thoreau wrote one hundred and fifty years ago.

The receptionist in the senator's office did nothing extra to make me feel at home, as they had in Williams's office. There was no welcome-weary-traveler-from-our-faraway-home greeting. Perhaps this was due to the rolled up maps under my arm.

I was informed that I could speak with an aide. They did not say whether the senator was indisposed, and I didn't ask — I didn't want to appear ungrateful.

Lynx, back in the cedar jungles, motionless, with stripes of light swatching their faces. Grizzlies. I had made it into the interior, on their behalf, and now I didn't want to make a fuss?

What I wanted was irrelevant, I reminded myself as I rose to greet the aide. He was a big man and though I had come in good faith, I sensed in the first few seconds that our electricities were not right.

Still, I thought, it's a thing we can work through. For the good of the land. For the good of Montana.

"Well, the prodigious writer of postcards," the aide said, and perhaps now I should take responsibility for our unfortunate first meeting, for this rankled me — I let it rankle me. I realize now how tense I was, how humorless and intent. It's true I had written a lot of postcards, but I had written a shitload of four- and five-page letters, too, to which they also had not responded.

I see now that maybe it was my fault — that maybe I took his words the wrong way. Maybe he didn't mean to sound snide or uncaring. Maybe I just heard wrong.

We got into an argument right away. I began showing him my maps of roadless areas, and overlaid a map showing the movements of radio-collared grizzly bears in the valley. It was a damn-near perfect 100 percent overlay: the bears stayed hemmed in by the roads as if the roads were strung with electric fence. I thought it was a remarkable piece of data: startling testament to the need to keep from further carving up these last sanctuaries for a few more weeks' worth of timber.

But we hit a philosophical snag right away.

"The presence of grizzlies is not necessarily indicative of wilderness," the aide said. "A grizzly does not necessarily make a piece of woods *wilderness.*"

I fell into the trap. "Well, no. . . ." I agreed, "but there's everything else living in those woods too — the whole matrix of it, still linked — the wolverines, elk, fishers, martens, wolves, caribou. . . ." — and on I went, agreeing that wilderness was not any one thing, but the whole of a place.

But a grizzly in Yaak *is* wilderness. In the Yaak, like nothing else, they're an indicator species: the first to leave, once an ecosystem is damaged. If the great bear is still living in the Yaak, then so too are all the other species below it.

But I got hung up in this grade-school semantics debate, right from the get go.

"The wild things still live there," I said. "Any basic conservation biology textbook will tell you that 100,000 acres is the minimum required for the preservation of a core population of large carnivores. We've still got about 150,000 acres in the Yaak if you keep them all linked together." I showed him the archipelago, the doughnut-around-the-hole; like the rings around Saturn, the roadless areas in Yaak are still connected. They may look like a heart shot through with a lifetime of adrenaline — a thing riddled with pockmarks — but they are still nonetheless tenuously connected, still pumping the wild.

I had one last question for him, before I left. It came as only an afterthought: some whisper, some spirit from the woods, roused me to ask it.

"Have you ever seen the Yaak?" I asked.

"No," he said, "I never have."

I reeled out, feeling kidney-kicked. Feeling the eyes of the wolverines, up in the autumn mountains; feeling the elk pause, as they drifted as a herd down into lower country, anticipating the snows of November. Thinking, perhaps, *Well, he tried.* We all have to make it on our own — that's a rule of nature. But I'm trying to buck it — I'm trying to believe that anyone who hears about this valley, and the complete disregard with which its wilderness has been treated in the past — the scandal of this omission, and the continued taking-without-giving — will be moved to help. I absolutely believe it, and can see it as clearly as a candle flame.

I can see letters raining down on members of Congress, the Forest Service, and big timber companies — enough to change, enough to stir them. I can see the letters coming like coal oil poured down the chimney, exploding into flames when they hit the embers, scattering the cabin's occupants; I can see Congress running out into the night, into the snow, trying to get out from under the flaming letters.

I reeled out onto the concrete streets. My world of gravel roads, and dirt roads, with the canopy of trees high above — roads like shady tunnels, with the gold larch needles blanketing them like a carpet, like the golden roads of heaven — seemed very far away.

Of course we know what happened. Pat Williams stood up

for the Yaak — passed his bill through the House, about two million acres of protection to begin with, statewide — over 150,000 acres in the Yaak, including a McIntire/Mt. Henry Conservation Reserve, which would have been dedicated exclusively to small loggers — and to planting trees that would, one day far into the future, finally grow tall and obliterate that heinous H-A-C above the McIntires' meadow — and the bill passed (though Pat had to fight off Don Young of Alaska like a bulldog; Young proposed amendments that would have specifically gutted acreage from the Yaak. . . .)

But of course even after that bill passed the House, they killed it in the Senate: they let it expire, unexamined. . . .

We must get back up.

The system's broken — or not broken, because it never really worked in the first place. There are good folks in the Forest Service — great people — but up high, where the gears turn, the power benefits only a few. The counties, receiving a 25 percent commission on all timber cut from the federal lands in their county, all but encourage the multinational companies to come in, cut the forests, and then get out as fast as possible, without doing any value-added work that would employ more laborers. In fact, it's in the counties' short-term *interest* to get the raw logs out as quick as possible — just cut 'em and get 'em out and cut more.

You could employ far more workers in a chair-making business, using the same amount of wood required for one worker to simply cut that tree; you could make that tree last for days, rather than seconds. You could help ease unemployment on a long-term basis, and you could save these last magical forests of Yaak and still provide the county with a base of support, out of all the revenues saved from unnecessary road construction into these last forests.

Why can't we have that? Why can't we have a business in Libby or Troy, in which the workers build bookcases and kitchen cabinets out of Yaak Valley bug-killed lodgepole? I do not believe that the truck drivers and sawyers cannot be taught to run a planer, to rout wood. To sand, screw, nail and finish. To *sustain*.

We'd still need truck drivers, and we'd still need sawyers.

But a value-added industry — to learn a craft — would employ more, and pay better. And you can't log forever — even if the woods stretched to eternity. It's like playing in the NFL — you only have so many good years before injuries do you in.

Meetings, meetings, another visit with the senator's aide — the Democratic senator. I drive over to Kalispell and bring with me several stacks of mail from people who want the last wilderness in the Yaak protected. There's easily enough to fill a wheelbarrow, so that's what I do: I empty the sacks into a red wheelbarrow, hundreds of letters overflowing, and push it in to the meeting.

The aide's face flushes. "What's this, a *prop?*" he demands, and I tell him, "No, it's *reality.*"

The Republican senator answers one of my letters. He says that he will do nothing that will sacrifice even one timber job in Montana. I write him back and ask him, But what if that one timber job costs eight other jobs somewhere else in the state — or sacrifices twenty-five potential jobs? He does not write back.

It's not the Forest Service's men and women in the field who are taking the wild away. It is up high, up where the money is leveraged — up where it leverages people's behavior — and we must leverage back our heritage, the woods, with votes, and with anger, if we do not have the dollars.

I don't believe Congress wants us making bookshelves and cabinets — they don't *want* us taking our time with the land. The timber industry that contributes to their election campaigns wants the quick cash flow, ship the rough logs to Japan, a dollar-on-the-hundred, and let *them* make the cabinets, then sell 'em back to us cheap, blowing our deficit even

further out of the water — no matter, keep the timber companies' cash flow going, propped up by subsidies into roadless
areas.

Am I explaining it clearly? Is anyone please angry enough
to write a letter? To write fifty letters, or five hundred?

It is a civil war, and if they have no honor for the land, then
how can you expect them to have honor or respect for you?

There must be some permanent wilderness refuges in the
Yaak — not a rotating system of open-and-closed roads, but
true wilderness. Roderick Mountain, for example — let its
name become forever synonymous with the wild. Let the
next generation know the wild.

It is a kind of church, back in these last cores. It may not be
your church — this last 1 percent of the West — but it is
mine, and I am asking unashamedly to be allowed to continue worshiping the miracle of the planet, and the worship
of a natural system not yet touched, never touched by the
machines of man. A place with the residue of God — the
scent, feel, sight, taste and sound of God — forever fresh
upon it.

One place, untouched by us. The wilderness. The harbor,
from which we came. *Home.*

The Dark-Eyed Owls

A COUPLE OF VALLEYS OVER from me, along the north fork of Montana's Flathead River, there lives a wildlife biologist, Rosalind Yanishevsky, whom I see from time to time. Dr. Yanishevsky is full of energy and wonder and strange knowledge — she seems to know *everything*. She has tangled dark brown hair and travels with a small white dog named Kachina. She has worked as a national park ranger and has taught classes in wildlife management and old-growth forest ecology. She has participated in research on the ecology of mule deer, wolves, woodpeckers and grizzlies. She seems happy in the world: especially when she is in the woods.

And she's in the woods a lot, these days — and on the road to and fro, working for the National Audubon Society in an effort to map the remaining ancient old-growth forests in Montana. Rosalind's hope is to correct and supplement the Forest Service maps before all that she intends to map is gone.

Foresters and biologists do not always agree, but they recognize that for a forested ecosystem to be healthy, old-growth stands should comprise a minimum of 10 percent of the forest's whole. But on my Kootenai National Forest, and adjacent to that, on Rosalind's Flathead National Forest (and I use the terms of possession as I believe any creature should, deer or owl or bear or man, who goes in and out of those forests), old growth comprises only 4 or 5 percent of the whole.

One of the reasons I like to be around Rosalind is that she doesn't despair. She doesn't panic when the environmental movement in this part of the world suffers loss after loss; she just keeps working harder, and offers an odd little smile, an incredulous, "Can you believe this?" laugh.

In the woods she stops to look around: raises her binoculars to the flash of wings through the trees, or looks down with an I've-never-seen-this-before interest at the smallest mushroom. Standing in the complexity of a towering old forest, Rosalind *looks;* and she wants the Forest Service to look, too, before it is too late. But she doesn't just want the Forest Service to save the remaining fraction of old growth — which will be gone in ten or twenty years, if it's not protected — she also wants "associated forests" set aside. These are mature stretches of woods that contain the components which will in turn, in twenty or fifty years, become old-growth forests. Historically, she suspects, some valleys in northwest Montana have had high percentages of old growth, and in any case forest managers would do well to provide themselves with a buffer beyond that 10 percent minimum.

A system of protection for these "associated forests" needs to be mapped and created. Stands contiguous to old growth can act as a corridor from one old-growth forest to another, thereby helping to prevent the genetic diversity of flora and fauna from becoming even more fragmented and isolated. Some *planning* is needed, some orderly system of sanity to keep together that which was never meant to be fragmented: and this may be why Dr. Yanishevsky exists in the world, I think; it's her present passion, her calling. To save us — if we will be saved. And if we won't — well, then, she'll at least try to save the owls. Her training starts at the level of the cell and extends all the way up to wolves, bears and giant trees. Man.

Over on what Rosalind calls the West Side — the Pacific Northwest — the failed Spotted Owl Bill of 1992 would have set aside from the timber industry that critical 10 percent of old-growth forest. (About the logging industry's and pork-barrel politicians' claims, generally unexamined by the media, that such protection will cost thousands of jobs and millions of dollars, Rosalind smiles and looks as if she wishes certain of her species had, if not more hunger for intellect, then at least more *imagination*. "It could be an opportunity for *more* jobs," she says — the creation of a new, labor-intensive industry of protective logging — selecting, pruning, trimming, measuring and evaluating the forests — *looking* at the trees — rather than the old machine culture of running amok, driving the giant Caterpillar up the hill and into the dark forest, erasing it, and erasing jobs for the next generation. . . .)

Although Rosalind finds herself hoping Oregon and the rest of the Northwest can pass meaningful ancient forests protection bills, she understands that the jaws and eyes of the timber beast will rotate accordingly to gaze across the line to Montana, where there is no protection of ancient forests.

She tells me they will be looking to Montana to make up for whatever is protected over there.

Rosalind understands *processes:* causes and effects. And that's the way it played out. The Clinton administration had their timber summit in the Northwest, and decided to protect some spotted owl habitat over there; but now industry is robbing owl habitat in the Yaak — and elk and grizzly and trout habitat — to make up for Washington and Oregon's protection.

We drive up to a lovely area on the border called Rat Creek. It's the place through which the Yaak River first runs as it crosses over Canada. Administered by the Forest Service, there are many big larch trees to be found. A private timber company clearcut 160 acres they owned from an area adjacent to Rat Creek — and now, since Champion Realty (previously Champion Timber) doesn't want to wait another two hundred years for the trees to grow back, they have put it (along with all their other Montana lands, which have received similar cut-and-run treatment) up for sale to developers.

At the edge of Rat Creek there is a section of river bottom land, prime grizzly and elk spring and summer habitat, which the owner has staked with pink ribbons as he, too, gears up to subdivide and to sell. The trees between these two gutted lust pits are immense.

Wolves inhabit this place, and thousands of deer and elk, great gray owls, pileated woodpeckers, black bears and an occasional grizzly bear. The whole forest shakes, trembles with a magic; I know that *something's* up.

Tension is alive in this forest; one thing is trying to dominate another.

I think that it is the old, trying to dominate the new.

Rosalind and I walk down a game trail for perhaps half a mile, looking up at the trees and down at all the different mushrooms. I ask questions — "What kind of tree is this? What kind of tree is that? How old do you think that one is?" — and gradually I notice that Rosalind is going slower and slower.

We're in what she calls a "subalpine spruce and fir zone," a place where larch, and shaggy, sharp-needled spruce trees grow strong beside flat-needled fir trees (Douglas firs have one needle-pod growth tip at the end of each twig, while the subalpine fir has three growth tips). I begin to see why Rosalind has stopped here. I'd been looking forward to showing her the even bigger larches further up the trail, but it soon becomes apparent that this is a better place for an examiner.

"The Forest Service doesn't want trees set aside for biological diversity," she says. She's standing in one spot, looking all around, studying. A big fire came through here she guesses about one hundred years ago, sparing only the larch due to their thick bark. The almost as tall but smaller-diameter lodgepoles shot up after that, and together these two species provided shade for the next successional stage, the fir and the spruce.

Hardly moving, Rosalind points out hemlock and cedar — the hemlock's needles green on top but shiny-silver beneath, almost aluminum-looking — a feathery look.

"This is a very diverse forest," she notes, taking three steps to a grand fir. And beyond it, there's juniper; a white pine (five needles to a bunch). She's sure the lodgepole came in after the larch, working its way up between the fire-surviving larches; the lodgepoles have no limbs for a long way up, indicating they had to grow a long way before they could reach the sun.

"Larch trees can get two to three times this size, if you'll let them," Rosalind says: a dizzying prospect. There is one monster larch tree that is definitely an old-timer, and we step over to measure it. She asks me to guess the diameter first, from a distance. I squint and imagine the great tree cut — I pretend I've lucked onto it in a slash pile while out cutting firewood — and make a guess of forty inches. Rosalind nods. "Pretty close," she says.

We stretch the tape measure four feet up to "breast height," then wrap the tape measure around the tree's circumference at that height. We're going to calculate the DBH — diameter-at-breast height — and to get the diameter we divide the circumference by pi and come up with 42.3 inches. A good, big tree. This one, Rosalind says, is some kind of veteran — maybe two or three hundred years old.

Rosalind is a mix of scientist and romantic, an ideal mix of microscope-squinter and world's-wonder wide-eyed gawker. Politician and rebel, she earns her living by numbers, swims through them as a trout through water — and she acknowledges that there are different numerical definitions for old growth (moisture regime, slope aspect, tree species and so on). In a subalpine spruce-fir forest such as the one we're in, she says, a general working definition might be fifteen trees per acre with a diameter greater than twenty inches. But that's the office part of her, the computer grids.

"There's so much," Rosalind says. "You have to look at

everything: light patches through the canopy, amount of nutrients on the ground, soil and logs in terms of decay, nesting
trees, snags. . . .

"It's close to being old growth," she says, looking around.
"Maybe in fifty years."

Larch makes the best nesting cavities for birds because the
outside bark is so resistant to rot, and yet the tops of the
biggest larches are prone to breaking off — often intercepting
lightning bolts, as they rise so high into the sky. These strikes
of lightning allow moisture and fungus to enter the heartwood and rot it from the inside; the end result (before the tree
falls, returning to earth) is that there is a nice protective shell
around a soft home for hole-dwellers.

Rosalind is reentering her scientist-state; leaving the quali-
tative, which is usually where the poets play, and coming
back into the realm of the quantitative. She steps over to a
patch of grand fir that is growing in a cluster around a lodgepole pine. Researchers have discovered that the yew tree of
this region grows in similar clusters. The yew has been very
important in testing for anticancer properties — an ingredi-
ent in the yew called Taxol has shown great success. The yew
grows in isolated communities, or families — and one stand's
Taxol production, Rosalind says, "can vary as much as ten-
fold. But they're cutting it all, without measuring," she says.
"They can wipe out an important genetic strain."

Rosalind frowns, and then tells of a friend hired by the
Forest Service to do "stand exams" — inventorying the diversity and quantity of various species, as required by law. It's
a pleasant enough job under normal circumstances — I
think of how good it felt to enumerate, record, *preserve*, even
if briefly, that one larch — 42.3 *inches* — but the trouble
Rosalind's friend has with the job is that they often do not
send him in to do stand exams until *after* they'd already
decided to cut, making his measurements meaningless.

"It's pretty disgusting," Rosalind says.

"Strangely enough, the Forest Service has destroyed the
records," she adds. "We try to examine the historical timber-

stand exam database — but after about six years, the Forest Service dumps their files. It's a little like George Orwell, or Lenin — destroying the past, and rewriting the future. They're saying to us, *What old growth? What old growth was here? Prove to me there was old growth here.*"

Later in the day we're still along the Canadian border, up by the Yaak cemetery, looking at more larch. The trees in the immediate area are almost-for-sure-safe: not from any written legislation, but from the simple and unspoken decency that it's not nice to run amok with chain saws in a cemetery; not nice to fell trees on the headstones.

The afternoon wind lifts and stirs the highest branches far above us. "I like that," Rosalind says, smiling, looking down at the little cemetery. "People fertilizing the trees, when they're through living."

These are *big* trees; we see several all around us that would measure at least forty inches DBH. She mentions that she's asked the Forest Service to include categories in their old-growth surveys for how many trees per acre (and what kind) measure more than thirty-inch DBH, but they're not interested in measuring forty-inch trees. "They say, 'Oh we hardly ever find trees like that anyway,'" she adds sadly. "All they want to do is confirm whether or not the tree meets the seventeen-to-twenty-one-inch minimum."

Rosalind pokes around the base of a larch tree. Big larches typically accumulate great mounds of detritus at their base — detritus that is home for all kinds of mycorrhizae and bacteria, the kind of stuff that only the rest of nature (and scientists like Rosalind) can understand and appreciate.

I notice she's going slower and slower again. It's so unlike our nature, I think, to move that slow; when I get into open woods my tendency is to hurry along. . . .

She begins pointing out old-growth components once again. "Conchs," she says — "tree ears." Just above us, in one of the lower branches, there's some *Alectoria* — the lime-green caribou lichen that woodland caribou would utilize were there any caribou left to feed on it. (Rosalind found caribou hair over near Glacier National Park in 1985; she suspected that's what it was, sent it in to the state lab, and sure enough, one had been through there.)

There's a big larch tree not too far ahead of us, down in a shady ravine, and I head toward it eagerly, like some kind of hunter, anxious to measure it: as if to lay claim to it. But Rosalind's entering micro-creep, and thinking about it now, I wonder what it must be like for her, in the woods, to be able to see so much — to see almost everything?

I would like to learn more, but understand that I'm going to have to move slower.

"Come back here and look at these lichens," she says.

I turn and go back to where she's crouched, looking at the underside of a fallen tree that leans down the hill. "It looks at first like there's just one lichen growing here, but you can see that there's two," she says.

I feel like nodding and saying Yes, Yes, now let's go measure that rascal over there (before he gets away?), but Rosalind's definitely in micro-creep — she's touching the two lichens, which are similarly colored and textured — only their patterns are different — one ornate, even baroque, and the other more clustered symmetrically — and so I, too, touch the lichens.

Now we're ready to go, I think. I touched the damn lichens.

I want to see *old growth*.

She gazes down the length of the tree.

"Even the way a tree dies adds to the diversity of the forest," she says. "If it breaks off high" — if it snaps, so that it sags to the ground like a lean-to — as opposed to 'pit-and-mound', where the root system comes up with the tree, creating more soil perturbation — "or if it breaks off too low." Something like that affects, I realize, all that will follow, forever after.

How the tree dies matters too in that if it falls pointing downslope, it'll be elevated only a little bit off the ground, providing for quicker nutrient fixing back into the soil. But if it falls across-slope, it will provide access for animals to walk across, above the deep winter snows.

"It makes a difference if it falls parallel to or opposite the slope," Rosalind says, her gaze still focused on the slender dead tree, "because it will cast different shadows on the ground, which then creates different growth patterns. . . .

"It bothers me," she says, turning toward me as though I would have the answer. "How can we do better than nature?"

We take one step away from the fallen tree, one of a dozen fallen trees around us. She stoops to examine a dark, pretty, waxy-leafed plant, *Pipsissewa* — prince's pine. "They need the larches' mycorrhizal fungus too," Rosalind says. Suddenly, I see, there's *Pipsissewa* all around us.

The woods are very quiet, as if agreeing.

We take another step toward the enormous tree I've had my eye on. "Orchids," Rosalind says, pointing, and then, "Queen's Cup — the one with the blue berry. It's an indicator plant of an old-growth forest, too."

I all but dash the last twenty yards to the tree, stopping, though, en route to look briefly at black bear scat. When I pick it up to ask what she thinks it is, Rosalind is horrified, not realizing I meant, Did she know whether it was black bear or grizzly scat. She seems to think that I consider it an old-growth *delicacy*. I know scat and muscle, she knows orchids and slippery clean meiosis. . . .

The tree I've all this time wanted to look at has a fifty-four-inch diameter at breast height. We spend a long time circling it, examining the thick great scales and ridges of bark. Forty or more feet above us, the trunk branches into three trunks, like a god.

"There's a little bird called the brown creeper," she says quietly, "that nests in the bark of giant larch trees like this one" — laying its eggs where one of the fist-sized scales of bark has half-exfoliated, a peeled-back place that allows the bird to wedge itself between the trunk and the flakey bark.

"It makes a hammock for the bird," Rosalind says, pointing to one such piece of bark where a small bird could lay one or two small eggs. "They live there and feed only by going *up* the tree with their curved bill, feeding all the way up, probing the bark for insects."

She looks around and I have the thought that, for the second, she's looking at the forest not through the eyes of a research scientist, or woods-walker, or anything like that, but through the eyes of a brown creeper: a bird.

"We need to save the best of what's left," she says. "You have to look at the landscape. If there's nothing else out there but lodgepole — then this, a diverse forest, becomes of immense value." She's talking about not just diversity of age, but of species. Even a *young* forest is rare these days, if it has diverse species within it. She blinks, pauses as if switching languages, and tries to explain it more clearly.

"Rather than being black-and-white about it, I've tried to encourage the Forest Service to come up with some sort of relative ranking system for what's left" — a system, says Rosalind, "based not just on *numbers*, but on what we have *left*; on what's *rare*."

At our third stop, at dusk, up in the Spread Creek drainage — the great divide that has provided not only for the vast majority of Montana's historic (and present-day) caribou sightings, but which has been of historic importance as a grizzly corridor — we stand below a dark cedar jungle watching a red sunset over the northwest peaks. For just how long will this view remain? And Spread Creek?

"How *can* we do better than nature?" Rosalind had asked.

Down below an owl begins to hoot. The woods are still except for the peace that seems to be sliding off the ridges as evening cools.

"Nobody listens to the importance of dead trees," she says.

When the owl hoots again, Rosalind smiles and says, "Maybe a barred owl — one of the dark-eyed owls." She smiles wider, listening to what is left of the forest.

This Savage Land

YOU CAN SEE THE GUYS from the city getting a bit funny-eyed, when Tim and I walk down to the put-in carrying a chain saw. It's raining hard, pouring off the brims of our caps, and they think it's a practical joke — the four-weight fly rod in one hand and the Stihl 034 Super (with extended bar) chain saw in the other. They're so polite, these guys from the East — famous writers, famous fishermen and world travelers — that they don't know whether they're being had or not, but they don't want to risk hurting our feelings, so they just huddle in the rain and puff cheerily on their cigars and stare through the drizzle at the damp woods pressing in from that riverside wall of green. Mist is rising from the river. Even the name itself sounds somehow terrible and sharp, *Yaak*, like the sound a hatchet might make, cleaving flesh and then bone, and perhaps they think, well, why not a chain saw?

I am not a fisherman, but the guide, Tim, my friend, has invited me along. The fishermen are dressed elegantly, ready for a bit of sport. I am wearing my old, stained overalls, ragged steel-toed boots, and I'm acutely aware of being half a foot shorter than any of these lanky, graceful gents — Tim, Tom, Charles, Dan and Chris. Actually, Chris is from Utah, Dan is from South Dakota, and Tom is from Jackson Hole, Wyoming — but from a Yaak standpoint, this qualifies them as easterners. Charles is from Nova Scotia. We have two drift boats and a raft with us, and when I climb into one of the boats with my chain saw, I think they are also acutely aware of my stumpiness, and with the saw, and climbing in awkwardly — not knowing much about boats — I do not feel like a fellow fly-fisherman, but like a pirate.

How gentlemanly are they? Dan hunts gyrfalcons in Saudi Arabia with princes. Charles and Tom and Chris own more bird dogs than I have empty aluminum cans in the plastic bag behind my barn. They hunt red deer in Mongolia, wild boar in Europe, and now they've come to the Yaak to fish in the rain for tadpole-sized brook trout while some troll rides along with them scouting for firewood.

"Got enough gas?" Tim asks me. "Got your saw tool?"

I nod. Tim goes over to the fishermen and asks them what kind of flies they have, and what size. Charles, Dan and Chris answer him dutifully; only Tom thinks to question authority. "Does it really matter?" he asks, and Tim looks surprised, then says, "No, they'll probably hit anything."

There is so much about fly-fishing that I do not understand, but I know enough to recognize that Tim is a great guide, so great that he does not have to be a snob. The river doesn't get too much traffic, due to the multitude of tiny unsophisticated fish that will never be anything other than tiny. Then there's the matter of the long winding flat stretches of river, and, as the gentlemen visitors are beginning to see, there is throughout the valley the vague and uncomfortable sense that the locals — us — may be watching from behind the bushes. The locals have some other-ness that is not easily defined, and which is not relaxing to visitors.

We didn't move up here to be around crowds, which may bring up the question of why I am then mentioning this river in the first place, this slow-moving water of dull-witted fingerlings. (I am tempted to tell you that Yaak is the Kootenai word for carp, or leech, or "place of certain diarrhea." It truthfully means *arrow*, but could also double to mean *rain*.)

Tim and I spend a good amount of time at other periods of the year hiking in the mountains, looking for antlers, looking for bear dens, looking for huckleberries, and in the winter, rattling deer and chasing elk — and then after that, grouse again, in the snow, in December, with our beautiful, talented dogs, and after that, ducks. . . .

On these trips, year in and year out, Tim and I go round and round in our anguish: do we keep silent about this hard-logged valley, or do we pipe up plaintively, make little cheepings, like killdeer skittering along the shore? We really don't care for the tourist hordes to come gawk at the clearcuts, or come feel the blue wet winds — to eat a cheeseburger at either of the local bars, to stand in the parking lot and marvel at the menagerie of woods-hermits-come-to-town-on-Saturday, as if a circus is parading past: gentle hippies, savage government-loathers, angry misanthropes, romantic anarchists, and a few normal people who in their normalcy appear somehow odd. Surely they are masking some great aberration. And those are the ones who come to town — who venture out into the light of day! The rest of us like to hide.

There is a certain duct-tape mentality that pervades this place. I'm not sure why, unless it's simply that things break a lot. It hasn't infected Tim yet and I guess after seven years if it were going to, it would have. He's neat and precise and does his job, finding fish and wild game, in an orderly, calculated fashion. But many of the rest of us tie socks over our broken windshield wipers, for instance, rather than venturing into town to get new wiper blades. We try to keep three of everything: one that runs, one for parts and one for a backup, if there's not time to switch our parts. But usually there's time.

We get our food, our meat and berries, from the land, and our produce from our gardens: root crops, which can stand the eternal cold. Blue smoke rises from chimneys year-round. The scent carries far in the humidity, in the drizzle.

The grizzlies aren't any problem up here; what will get you are the leeches, blackflies, mosquito hordes, and eight species of horseflies (including one the size of the head of a railroad spike, whose bite is like being nipped by a fencing tool.)

I don't mean to be falling over myself so much, rolling out

the welcome mat. The logging trucks keep coming and going. They drive hard and fast, and they will run your tourist-ass off the cliffs in a minute, then laugh about it.

Tim's livelihood depends, more or less, on bringing people into the valley. But like most of us, he thinks it would be nice to keep Yaak the way it is, or even better, to have it somehow reappear as it was five or ten or twenty years ago. (Twenty-eight years ago, there was only one road through the valley. Now there are over a thousand miles of road, and counting. And still not one acre of protected wilderness.)

Relax. I'm not going to lay the enviro-eco-rap on you. Or will try not to. I'm trying to kind of place you in Tim's position.

In order to keep living here he needs people to ride in his boat and cast flies, just as some must keep building roads, or cutting trees, to keep living here. But when there are no fish, and no more trees, and when every last mountain has a road onto it . . . then what? Do we learn semiconductor manufacturing in the evenings?

Tim has, among other guides, a funny reputation in some respects, as he doesn't always seem like he wants to be a guide. There's very little telephone service or electricity in the Yaak, and it's a long damn way to any airport — more than three hours to Kalispell, four to Spokane, five to Missoula. Phone service and electricity are erratic up here. Tim's answering machine has some electronic glitch — some pulse of the wild, perhaps, that it has picked up from the soil itself, as the coils and cables snake just beneath the skin of the earth — which causes it to shut off on the incoming message after your first six words, so you'd better choose them well.

Other guides joke (though I get the sense they really believe it, too) that it's something Tim does on purpose — that not so deep down, he doesn't want new clients. Or that maybe he wants them, but then feels guilty about wanting them. The way I feel guilty, about writing about this wet buggy valley.

So Tim gambles that the people he introduces to the slow

snag-infested water will fall in love with the valley and work to keep it from being further abused, and I make the same gamble, continuing to write about it.

We intend on this trip to use the chain saw for snags. It's a little river, and trees fall across it regularly, blocking your passage. In other places, the deep river suddenly splits into four braids, each only a few inches deep, so that you may have to portage if you don't pick the right one. Also, there is a guy up here who lives along the river and hunts with a blowgun. He likes to hide in the bushes and shoot tourists. At first you think it's just another horsefly. But then you develop a headache, and then you grow sleepy. You put the oars down and lie back in the boat for a minute, just to nap, you think. . . .

If you did come all the way up to this last tiny river, it could be deadly to not use Tim for a guide. And if you did come, there'd be that vow of undying commitment we'd ask you to sign: to fight forever, hard and passionately for this wet people-less place, on behalf of all wildness — to fight to keep it as it is, at least.

Of course, we're asking you to take that vow anyway, whether you come or not. For the grizzlies, wolves, woodland caribou, elk, and wolverines that live back in what remains of the wet jungle, and which you would never see anyway, if you were to come up here, as they've all become almost totally nocturnal. And for those eight species of horseflies, which have not.

I guess you're waiting to hear about the river, and about fish, and here I am yowling about the wilderness. But it seems so simple. We have only three congressmen for the whole state. There is no designated, protected wilderness in the valley. If everyone who liked or favored clean water and the notion of a dark secret place, with feisty little fish and moose and great blue heron rookeries and dense spruce jungles — if everyone who liked these things would begin a correspondence with the three congressmen concerning the Yaak, I think they would finally come to understand that, timber budget or not, the remaining roadless acres in the Yaak should be protected.

Back to the gents. It's an honor to be in their company. They don't care if they catch fish or not. They just enjoy being out-of-doors, and in a new land. Since childhood they've probably caught seven million fish, cumulatively. Every fish mouth in the world is sore from their hooks. Today they're enjoying just being alive. They're standing in the rain.

When we set off, I'm in Tom's raft. Dan and Charles are in their own boat, and Tim's ranging ahead of them in his boat, with Chris, like a bird dog. The guys stop at the first gravel bar and get out and wade near the line where some fast water meets some slow water, and begin casting pretty casts into the line.

But nothing. Tim rows on, as if knowing there aren't any fish there. Tom watches Tim disappear around the bend and starts to say something, but doesn't. We lean back and watch Charles and Dan cast. If they catch something, maybe we'll rig up. Charles, Dan, Chris and Tom have been on a road trip across Montana — they've fished nine rivers in nine days. This is the tenth, and Charles (from Nova Scotia, and formerly, New England, and before that, the South) is raving about what a beautiful, perfect little trout stream it is: how it reminds him of when he was a child, and was first learning to fish on brook trout rivers.

He's tired of all the muscle rivers of the past nine days and, believe it or not, of all the muscle-fish. He's content to cast and let his line drift and smoke his cigar in the rain.

The Yaak is a tiny river, but an important one, especially with the loss of the upper Kootenai River (and the now-extinct Ural Valley) to the wretched dam that formed Lake Koocanusa, in order to send more juice to California. The Yaak flows from four forks down into what remains of the Kootenai, a river that reminds one of the Mississippi. And the

Kootenai then flows, Yaak-laden, into the Columbia, where it becomes fragmented by dams — lakes where salmon once ran wild.

It boggles my mind to stand in one of the cedar forests high in the mountains of Yaak and watch a creek — say, Fix Creek — go trickling down through the forest, a foot wide and a foot deep — and to picture it being received by the Yaak, and then by the Kootenai, and then by the Columbia, and then by the ocean.

This is my home.

I know that in writing about a river, you're supposed to concentrate on the fish — and then, narrowing the focus further, upon the catching of them.

Tim's a good guide, a great guide. He can find you a big deer. It's not real good elk country — too many roads, not enough security areas, according to biologists — but he can give it the best shot of anybody. His maniacal sense of sportsmanship has altered me. We shoot only about every tenth grouse. *Too slow!* we'll cry to each other when a bird crosses the other's path, or *Young bird!* or *Old bird! Let 'er go!* — year by year increasing our ridiculous standards, out of our love for this savage place, until a grouse just about has to be going 90 mph downhill through doghair lodgepole in the rain for us to get the green light.

I wonder sometimes if I in turn influence Tim with my duct-tape-ness. We often forget to be hard-core hunters. While hunting with him, I carry plastic Ziploc bags and collect bear scat to give to the biologists for DNA testing of genetic vigor. While drifting the Yaak we stop and search for pretty river rocks. We collect water samples. When we're out together on the water, we do just about everything but fish. Tim tells me the names of the insects, teaches me to cast, but time and time again I skew the subject, and talk about baseball or football — about his moribund, erratic Patriots or my choke-bound Oilers.

If it's spring, we discuss the autumn; if it's fall, we discuss the spring. In the summer and fall, when it rains, we talk about how nice it is to be dry.

I jabber a mile a minute, and never about fishing, and rarely about hunting, but always, it seems, about the valley.

Tim rows in closer to shore to examine the skeleton of a bull moose that has drowned in one of the deep holes, and tells me about the time he caught an eight-inch rainbow by dragging a nymph through the moose's algae-hued skeleton ten feet down — the fish rising from the pelvis to take the nymph and then trying to turn back to the sanctuary of the vertebrae, but no luck. Tim reeled the fish in, though after a moment he gently released him.

I know you're not going to travel this far to catch an eight-inch rainbow. But maybe you can travel over to your desk and pick up a pen. Sort through the papers until you find a stray postcard and write the three congressmen.

The five gentlemen and I drift. It's a pleasure to watch them cast. The word Tim uses to describe the river is "intimate." The Kootenai is where he makes his money (as much as any guide ever makes, which is to say, not much), and the Yaak is what he saves for a few special lazy days of the year.

It's still raining, but slants of light beam through the foglike clouds along the river; the fog hangs in the tops of the giant spruce and cedar and fir trees. These trees are a function of the thin soil, tight gray clay over glacial cobble, and the soil is a function of the bedrock, which is in turn a function of the earth's belly, the earth's anatomy — what she desires to belch up here in this spongy, lush river country.

At times it is more of a creek than a river, like a child's ride in a raft through an amusement park, with the theme of "jungle." You can reach out and touch either bank, in places. Deer rise from the tall grass to peer at you, only their heads visible over the banks: big-eyed does, wide-ribbed in pregnancy, and bucks in velvet nubs.

"Short casts," Tim tells the occasional wanderer who inquires about fishing the Yaak with him. "Short casts. Intimate. You can see everything. You can see the moss growing on the rocks. You can see the caddis nymphs, the stonefly nymphs, crawling under their rocks. You can see the fish. Intimate," he says.

Purple anvil-shaped thunderheads tower behind us, rising between the forested mountains all the way to the outer arc of the atmosphere, and perhaps beyond: we are so wet, so drenched, and it is still raining so steadily, that perhaps it is raining on the moon.

We pass beneath an old wooden covered bridge. Soon we will be out in the riffles where the rainbow trout leap. Black and silver, they look like anchovies.

We trade off riding in different boats and rafts, to chat; to get to know one another. It's not about fishing. It's about being in the Yaak. It's about feeling the magic of all the little feeder creeks, cedar streams, not so rich in nutrients, but rich in magic, emptying into the Yaak's little belly. Later in the summer there will be a drought, whose only saving grace will be that the temperatures never get too hot; though the river will drop drastically, lower than it's ever been measured in white man's history; and in August, fires will move through on the south-facing slopes, cleaning out the underbrush, the dried-up buffalo berry that has grown up following old logging operations, and cleansing some of the lodgepole stands up high of pine beetles. And in September, on Labor Day, as on every Labor Day, the rains will return, extinguishing the fires, and beginning to give ease to the suffering creeks, and the fish will begin gathering at their mouths, readying to spawn in the fall rains, as they have almost every year through the millennia.

(Tim, a lover of waters, has moved up and down practically every creek in northwestern Montana, every backwater beaver-slough he can find, taking pictures of the occasional freak brook trout or the incredibly rare westslope cutthroat. Not surprisingly, those creeks that haven't been streamside- or headwaters-logged tolerate the droughts much better than the clearcut stretches.)

We pass beneath giant cedars. A few more fish. I hook a ten-inch rainbow, which will be the heavy of the day. Wild rainbows, and wild westslope cutthroats, and the gorgeous little brook trout. It's not unusual, Tim says, to catch all three; while just below, in the Kootenai, the bull trout breathing water breathed by sturgeon, and each year these creeks get filled in with more and more sediment, get lower and lower, and each year the bulls wait to make their heroic runs one more time.

We talk about books, we talk about politics, we talk about dogs and food and friends and assholes. We talk about the ocean and about Africa and about childhood. Charles is smoking a pipe now, and the smoke mixes with the fog. These damn little fish keep hooking themselves on our casts. Some of us put our rods down and just ride. The water turns dark, deep. Like any small river, the Yaak can be overfished by a single guy intent upon only meat, and in the past, it has been. The days of big fish in big holes are no longer with us, but because the river's small, the little fish still hide behind almost every rock.

Later on, at supper, we'll hit the five gents up for letters to save this wild green place. We'll tell them how, in all the years, there's never been a single acre of wilderness protected; how the international timber companies have long had their way with this forgotten place. We'll tell them that it's time to hold the Montana delegation responsible. Tim will discuss the Kootenai, and the Libby Dam operations, at length. The sign-up sheet will be passed, and the new letter writers recruited before dessert is passed out — if they want any dessert. A trade; the army, the small battalion, growing by four.

All that will come later. Right now it's time only for river intimacy. Green drakes begin to rise from the water, and Tim is overjoyed: in seven years, he's never seen them on the Yaak. He wants to believe that the river is recovering. We're drifting through a meadow now, where every year before cattle had grazed, but this year the cattle are gone, and the willows have grown at least a foot, and the green drakes are swarming, landing on our arms as if trying to tell us things.

A purple thundercloud drifts up the river to meet us — lashes us with stinging rain. We laugh like school kids walking home in a storm. We come around one corner — aspens, white pine, alder, ash, all clinging to a rock outcrop — and turn into a cool dark tunnel of cedar and spruce. Another bend, and now an old spruce stretches across the little river, spiny limbs splayed everywhere, resting a few inches above the water and spanning it completely. The tree is so big that it must have been a giant before whites first moved into the valley in the early 1900s. It's probably fifty inches across; it's too low to go under, and too high for us to drag our boats up over it.

The current has quickened, here in this dark tunnel, and we back-paddle to avoid being drawn into the limbs and turned sideways. We're all aware of the furious, silent power of water, even relatively mild water — the strength of its mass — and the way things can turn bad quickly.

Carefully I climb up on top of the tree — thrashing through the maw of branches — and Tim anchors, and hands the saw up to me.

The saw's wet and won't start at first. We're a long way from anywhere. It's raining harder still. Finally the saw coughs, then ignites, with a belch of blue smoke and a roar, and I choke it back to a purr, then start blipping off branches to clear a working area. Sawdust showers all three boats, all five fishermen. The rain beating down quickly mixes with the sawdust to coat them all with a sodden paste. A bit of bar oil drips into the river, sending a heartbreaking iridescent rainbow downcurrent. So much for the pious talk of the afternoon.

I begin making my crosscuts in the huge tree. The roar is deafening. How will I be able to hear grouse flush this fall?

So much for intimate. The green wood sags. Our worst fear is of binding the saw, and I'm careful, but can't get beneath the log with the blade — not unless I put it under-water.

There's a creaking, and the log drops an inch, pinches the saw tight. Now we're screwed. We take turns clambering onto the log and pulling, wrenching and twisting — a fly-fisher-man's version of *The Sword in the Stone.* A fly-fishing guide's nightmare. Surely he's wondering why he brought me.

The rain lashes at us. Finally Tim, in the strength of des-peration, is able to free the saw. I start it back up. Nothing runs like a Stihl.

I'm standing in the bow of his new boat making a new cut, and making good progress, when a new sound begins to emanate from the saw, a splintery sound, accompanied by a certain bucking and vibration of the boat. *Ahh,* I think, *we're into the heartwood now.*

Out of the corner of my eye, I notice a new color of sawdust beginning to appear in the pile around our ankles: it's cream-colored, the same color as Tim's boat.

He's such a gentleman! "That's O.K.," he says, when I lift the saw and stare, aghast, at the cut in the gunwale: as if I aimed to sink us! "Just a ding," he says.

Tim doesn't belong up here, really. He's like those other four gents. He's too courteous, and too *professional.* I'm afraid of giving him my virus, the one that makes you fond of duct tape; afraid of infecting him somehow with a woods-piggish-ness, a kind of savagery that is not uncommon in Yaak. I want him to be immune from it: and so far, he is. His New Eng-land heritage, etc. I'd already torn up his truck; he'd parked it behind my old beater one day, and I backed into it. "Ah, that's O.K.," he'd said then, too. "Just a ding."

It's a different place, up here. There's certain roughness of spirit; a wildness. You can see it in the old cars and trucks, in all the rotting things. A certain endurance, a willingness to go on, even when a bit crippled up by hard times, by deep snows, or whatever. But Tim's a pro, and such a nice guy: I feel guilty, as if my looseness, my Yaakness, might cramp his style. As if the valley might cramp his style.

He loves it, too. At least as much as I do. I guess if he were going to turn into a savage, it would have already happened.

I finish the cut, avoiding the boat this time. The log drops with a crash, swings free; the current surges. New structure — a new hole for the worm fishermen. We pull up anchor and release ourselves through the slot, like salmon through a gate. The rain finally lets up; sunlight pours down the mountains. We enter long, slow water — flat water, with much rowing to be done. We're cold, chilled to the deep bone. Fresh sawdust floats downriver with us, preceding us for a mile or so.

Shadows deepen. There's one touchy moment when we come to a spot in the river where a man has draped a 220-volt electrical line across the river at neck level, as if to electroshock us; but it turns out he's only doing some welding on the other side of the river. In the dimness, we might not have seen it. Tim knows the man, is friendly with him, as he is with everyone. He gives the magic password, and the man lifts his cable high enough for us to go by unelectrocuted.

We take out in deepening, buggy twilight, slapping mosquitoes, and go up to the tavern to watch one of the basketball playoffs. Later we feast on wild game accompanied by wine and cigars and stories.

Driving home that night, Tim will tell me, he saw a lynx with only three paws cross the road; the fourth paw was raw and stumpy, probably from a trap. But Tim said he could tell by the way the lynx crossed the road that it still wanted to go on. It would rest up, Tim thought, and recover.

Healing

JUST ON THE OTHER SIDE of the valley, down at
the bottom of the summit — between Libby and the beginning of the valley — there is a small building, a place of
miracles, attached to the side of a garage barn. A sign out
front advertises it as the Sports Therapy Clinic. It's run by a
mother, Shirley, and her daughter, Connie. Part of their training, as I understand it — one of their specialties — lies in the
treatment, the massage, of horses; but if your back, or neck, or
anything, is hurting badly enough, they'll work on you, too,
and you can take it to the bank that if there is anyone who
can repair you — can piece you back together — it's them.
Their hands — strong enough to push a horse's entire hind-
quarter back into position — stretch and knead and twist and
torque your own puny hindquarters, and often you get the
feeling (read: *pain*) that they might be in some zone or trance
where all good artists go when they do their work, and that
they are working on your spine as they would that of a horse
or some other creature five times your size and more oblivious to pain.

These are not light touches, nor particularly pleasant ex-
periences — these sessions on the table. Sometimes it approaches torture. But you go there because it works. I
shouldn't be letting the cat out of the bag — shouldn't be
advertising the miraculousness of their work. In all my travels
I've never found anyone else who could fix my torn and

twisted back as well or completely as Shirley and Connie; what if people start coming to them from all over the world — what if overbooking leads to their being less accessible to our community?

Certainly, the wooded country, the community and the landscape around us, demands them — requires the miracle of them, as everything that fits in a place is a miracle. Log truck drivers, sawyers, hunters, fishing guides (all that boat-rowing) and deskbound, hump-shouldered writers alike need them in the world, in this community. In late winter, when the snow turns to ice and on any given day you can see a fair percentage of the people in Libby flat on their backs, spinning, having just fallen on the ice — as if you have stumbled into some strange town where a cult of break-dancers exists — ten or twenty people spinning on the sidewalks at a time, some days — the two women will sometimes work eight, even ten hours a day, nonstop, trying to put back together all the pieces: trying to rearrange the sheath of muscles, and the flows of blood and energy, which wrap each person's skeletal system.

There are charts and posters all over the walls of their little office: anatomical pathways of nerves, arteries, vessels, muscles, bones. . . . The way the tenseness in the left calf, for example, ties in, strangely enough, and transcribes itself to that pain behind the right shoulder blade. The way indigestion, or the pain in your lower abdomen, relates to the cramping in the arch of your foot. The way that when any one part gets too far out of balance, everything else shifts and tries to compensate but leads only to further unraveling and excruciating pain.

A wood stove keeps the office, the massage tables, melt-muscle warm, even at twenty below. Sunlight pours in through the old-glass windows. There's a creek across the road. Shirley's husband's family homesteaded here — no electricity, no phone, certainly no running water. She and her husband, Harold, raised four kids — Harold is a logger —

and the whole family of them, the history of them as well as the present tense of them, is *of a place*, as a tree is of a forest — and you find yourself wishing, selfishly of course, when Shirley works on you, that her hands, strengthened from working in the garden and on the horses, and on injured people, were not quite so *vital*.

Not that Connie is any less brutal.

Either of them will fix you.

Sometimes, as they work on you, they'll talk about the world — about *big* things — as if to somehow balance the toxicity and angst that must be coming out of your muscles. They'll work on anyone, on everyone — hard-core timber beasts and hard-core environmentalists alike, no matter — forgiving each of us our tensely wired human flaws — but personally speaking, you don't ever want to argue too much with them, about *anything*, when you're on the table, and if some topic starts to veer too closely toward significant disagreement, you try and change the topic to something like, say, the smell of roses, or the coming of spring. With one hand clutching the back of your neck as an eagle's talon clutches a rabbit, and the other hand similarly gripping your calf, you don't want to upset them: you want to keep them relatively calm and even-keeled.

They win all arguments on the table. "Well" — *ahhh!* — "yes, it's true" — *argh!* — "that maybe a *little* clearcut now and then" — *ohhh!* — "might not" — *aiee!* — "be too . . . bad" — *ahhh!*

They give instead of taking. It's incredible, the shared common ground the community has, just from the invisible braids of healing that are shared between us, from those of us who have visited them. They heal our physical imbalances, sculpt us back into who and what we should be, as I wish we could do — overnight, or in an afternoon — to the imbalances of the valley, and to the frictions that sometimes come up within the community.

The dark woods just up the road from their shop: the valley of big timber, valley of mystery, lying just over the summit.

There is this thing they do to your spine near the end of your session: they place their hand on a certain spot on your back and hold it there. Your senses fill. Oxygen roars into your ravaged muscles, though there is no sound. You can't hear a thing, not even your heart. You shut your eyes and you levitate, float there for a minute, maybe longer. Peace fills you.

Afterward, you walk outside, healed, ready to hurl yourself at the world again. Ready to forget the lessons of peace their hands have kneaded and woven back into you.

The crispness of the air, the smell of the mountains. The cry of a Stellar's jay — a flash of bright blue, flash of sun, and the sound of the creek. The drum of a pileated woodpecker working on a twisted, rotting snag. *These mountains.*

Fires

IT IS A WINDY DAY in mid-August 1994, and nearly all the inhabitants of Yaak have gathered in the log church that doubles as our community center. We've had bake sales in this place and we've voted here. Today an army officer, heavyset and dressed in camouflage, is here to tell us how to keep from burning to death. Outside, copper-colored smoke and sunlight blend into a fog that won't go away. The air feels as heavy around us as the lead apron that you used to wear during X-rays. The last really good fire that came through this valley was in 1910, and it burned from Spokane to Kalispell, an area of three million acres. The smoke was visible in Chicago.

Because of the lack of phone service in most of this valley, we are cut off from news of the outside world — which is usually how we like it — but today we're anxious to hear the weather report. We get one: high winds, possibly thirty-to-forty-mile-per-hour winds from the west, dry lightning and no precipitation.

Already the flames are sawing their way up the logged-over slopes of the Mt. Henry/McIntire country, chewing their way through dead lodgepole pine that the timber companies said they would log but didn't. (Instead they took the big green trees, spruce and larch.)

Closer to home, the flames move up the side of Lost Horse Mountain, leaping from clearcut to clearcut. The fires are on the south side of the river — a function of the spectacular lightning storms that moved down the valley late in July, and again on the fourteenth and fifteenth of this month, lighting certain trees in the forest like candles — tongues of lightning flickering and splitting the heavens open with white light, each one searching for the one tree, the one dry dead tree, with the itch, the specific itch, to be born again. During two nights in mid-August, more than 160 fires were reported on the Kootenai National Forest, and from that point, it was up to the wind to see if the fires would run (they almost always climb, rather than descend) and leave new life in their wake — or whether the order of rot and decay would be preserved for at least another year.

At night some of us drive to the top of Hensley Face, on the other side of the river — for now the "safe" side — and from there we look down at the valley and see the fires blinking yellow through the bed of smoke; fires blinking like a thousand flashbulbs, seeming sometimes strangely synchronized as breezes blow across them. It is like a vision of the underworld.

In the meeting, the army sergeant, who has fought fires before, though never in this valley, talks to us about the Fowler and Turner and Fish Fry fires, all of which are less than a mile from my home and, in his words, *really rocking.*

The firefighters have it down to a science, which is both reassuring and terrifying. They measure the humidities in combustible materials — *wood* — in advance of the fire, and they measure the per-acre volume of fuel. These measurements are then broken down into size categories: is the fuel comprised of twigs and branches, or limbs, or entire downed trees? It all matters.

Evacuation orders and alternate plans are discussed; we take inventory of who isn't among us. If the roads are aflame we'll meet in Gail's wide meadow along the river and hope helicopters can get through. I have doubts about that, as it seems smoke would pool in those places. It's the smoke that usually kills you, not the flames. We are instructed, if trapped, to lie down in the Yaak River or in a creek with a wet towel over our face.

The lecture is drowned out by the sometime sound of choppers and bombers cruising low over the woods. The helicopters pour onto the flames thousand-gallon buckets of water dipped from the river and lakes, and the bombers spray water or smoking trails of fire retardant. I wonder idly if the retardant is good for the soil — good for the watershed. More wind is coming, the sergeant says. There is a good chance the whole place could go, and go quick. We'll know within twenty-four hours. He wants us to be ready to leave in under five minutes' notice.

Despite dangers, most of us have stayed. It's an incredible pull — the bond to home, the bond to your place.

That afternoon I go to the mercantile to get extra gas, but it's closed. That would be a real bummer, I think, to be evacuating and run out of gas. Murphy's Law to the nth. A friend is sitting on the porch of the tavern drinking beer, a lot of it, and watching the hypnotic sight of a mountain on fire — the mountain right across the river.

"If we burn, we burn," he says.

I go home and head into the woods behind our house — up to the top of Zimmerman Hill, to peer down at the Okaga Lake fire, but I can't see anything for all the smoke. My wife is pregnant with our second child, and it occurs to me that this would be an even less opportune time than usual to get myself killed — to do something dumb — and so I turn and go down the safe, unburned side of the hill. On my way I encounter a curious thing: a covey of blue grouse ground-roosting, mid-slope, with a covey of ruffed grouse. I've never seen or heard of such a thing, and I consider whether the blue grouse have moved off their usual roosts up on the ridge because they know the fire will come over it. I wonder if they can feel it coming, like a tingle or an itch, through the soil and the rocks beneath their feet.

Down low, the deer have been moving at all times of the

day, looking dazed and confused; many of them stand mid-stream in the little creek.

I decide to begin moving some things out of the cabin — books, and family pictures. And as the road is still open, I decide to take my old Ford Falcon to the nearest town, Libby, before the road becomes crisscrossed with burning timbers and transformed into a hot-air wind tunnel of flame.

In Libby I'm stopped and given a citation because the car has a brake light out. I verbally abuse the arresting officer. Ash floats down on us onto our heads and shoulders, down onto the car itself, as we argue. He lives in the city, where it's safe.

The fires go out as they always do. The weight of their own smoke — the lack of oxygen, once they've used so much of it — the ennui of their own existence — often puts them out. Firefighters abetted the process, as did the rains that always come on Labor Day. By the time it was over, only 2 percent of the forest had burned, in varying degrees of intensity. I would have liked to have seen everyone go home right away — two thousand national guardsmen came to this shy valley from as far away as Alabama, Arkansas and Louisiana — a twentyfold increase in the social and cultural stress on the valley — but I have to say that for a couple of days I was glad that they were there.

All over the West, scientists as well as residents are trying to figure out how to apply this most basic truth: *the forests have to burn*. Suppression only makes forests lean more toward this truth. Many parts of the Yaak have changed from a once stable, fire-resistant system comprised largely of cedar-hemlock and larch to a more combustible mix of fir and lodgepole pine. In the past, the thick bark of older larch trees and the cedar's affinity for swamps have protected these two species. But now, the fir and lodgepole, without fires to keep them in balance, are encroaching into new territory, displacing these slower-growing, more fire-resistant species. Further stresses on the forest, beyond the cumulative stress of complete fire

suppression, include insect infestations of forests adjacent to gaping clearcuts, diseased blister-rusting white pine, and acid rain–weakened firs. All this adds up to what's called, ominously and accurately, fuel loading.

In the last three decades of fire suppression on the nearby Lolo National Forest, for instance, approximately one-tenth the volume of wood has burned than used to. Additionally, most fires in the past burned "cooler" because excess fuel was kept from loading up by the frequency of fires. Cooler fires spared many trees and left behind a diverse mosaic of burned and unburned species and age classes: different for each fire. The forests must have been seething with diversity, with suppleness — with health.

Today's fires — and we really haven't seen a truly big one — are burning hotter.

The timber industry has an answer, of course, and it isn't shy about touting it. All that autumn, ads blared over the radio saying that if the industry had been allowed to do more logging, the fires wouldn't have happened.

Never mind that about 70 percent of the fires on the Kootenai were in logged areas. Cut down all the trees, the timber industry seems to be saying, before they catch on fire.

Except: it is our past and present logging practices that have helped contribute to the very problem. Since in most logged-over areas there are not enough big dead trees left behind to rot slowly on site — to live out their cycle of rebirth — the soils on these public lands are becoming impoverished at rates so startling they often cannot even be measured. Sometimes soil is washed away following the clearcuts, while at other times it sprouts knapweed, hawkweed and thistles — grass-replacing noxious exotic weeds that are undigestible by big game.

The forest isn't always coming back on its own — not the forest type that the land has fostered naturally, has created. When trees are planted by man, at great expense, and using different species than the original, they are often weaker, more prone to disease and sun and wind. This can result in

early deaths and greater volumes of tree death — fuel loading — which can make a stand more susceptible to hot fires, rather than cool fires. The hot fires do further damage to the soil: and the remaining ashes from these hot fires often slump into the nearby streams and creeks, causing severe sedimentation.

It is out of balance. We need to reestablish order — and certainly, to keep our hands off the roadless areas, which are the true sources of and models for forest health. But the current Congress, greedy for all of the burned sticks, won't hear of it. They've declared an emergency, and to make sure industry can go in and cut all that wood before any of it returns to the soil, the way wood has been doing for roughly four billion years, Congress has passed a bill — written by timber companies — outlawing any environmental restrictions or regulations on salvage harvests.

Salvage in theory refers to dead trees, but it is defined in this bill as anything with the potential to burn, which basically covers any tree in the world. President Clinton vetoed this bill — it was a rider tacked on to the Budget Rescissions Bill — the first veto of his presidency. The Yaak — and the West — was granted one more year of life. Then, a month later, Clinton changed his mind, and the Yaak was again in danger.

The aerial photos of the aftermath of forest fires on the Kootenai tell an interesting story. The blackest areas — the fires' origins, in many instances, and places where they burned hottest — radiate from the edges of the big clearcuts and into the weakened, diminished forests. A favorite saying in the timber industry is "Clearcuts don't burn," but they do. The sun at the clearcut/forest interface scorches that area exceedingly, making it unnaturally dry, as do the strong winds now sweeping across the clearcut's lunar surfaces. These winds blow down excessive snarls of weakened timber around all edges of a clearcut, and pathogens and insects flood the woods through these new avenues.

Well, maybe, says industry, but the clearcuts hold their snowpack longer since they release most of their radiant heat back to space each night, without that pesky heat-trapping overstory. And it's true, they do. And then along about the first of June, about the time the streams and rivers have finally started to clear up from normal spring runoff, all the remaining snowmelt (and sediment) goes at once, in slumps and muddy gushes, rather than trickling slowly out of the old cool cedar woods, like a tap being slowly opened: the way nature, and springtime in the Rockies, is designed to work.

Old growth forests are simple in a way that a child can understand. The forests create their own healthy stable world, and maintain it. The thick bark of the oldest trees, and the way they shed their branches, almost coyly — almost *tempting* little grass fires to catch in those brush-tangles and limb-tangles, helps to keep the forest cool and clean and nutrient-rich, below.

All those old lichens hanging down from the oldest trees, hard-earned, are not just for show: if floating sparks land in them, the lichens flare up like a torch and then extinguish themselves, having used up all the surrounding available oxygen in that quick flush — leaving the tree almost totally unscathed.

Even the timing of the fire season in the West is a thing of great beauty and great health. The way the fires come, sometimes in July but usually in August — allowing just enough time to download some fuel and recycle some nutrients, but not so much that things get out of hand; in September, the rains come, turning the fires to smoldering embers, and in October and November the snows come, extinguishing them. Even larch needles carried by the autumn winds seem to be full of purpose.

One morning in October you wake up and there's a quarter- or half-inch mat of beautiful gold needles, and beautiful gold aspen leaves, spread all across the countryside. This golden blanket helps pin down the charred coals and ashes of

August, keeps too much of the ash from blowing away or slumping into creeks: this blanket speeds up the soil-making process — as much as that glacial pace can be helped along.

The interconnectedness of things. I'm all for prudent salvage logging, as long as it's not in roadless areas. But when a given industry asks to be put above or beyond the law, I get frightened, and angry. It is not the fires of autumn I fear. I respect those — but they are nature's way, and can be no more controlled than the wind or the rain. They're part of the weather of the West. To keep clearcutting forests or entering roadless areas under the guise of preventing forest fires (isn't suppression what got us in trouble in the first place?) is like going into the forest with gallon-sized watering cans during a drought. It's just not going to work. What we're dealing with is too big. And ever worse than not working — it makes things worse — more imbalanced, more brittle.

The fire season has taught me a lot, has taught me a new way of looking at the woods. Now when I go for a walk, or climb a forested mountain, I'm very conscious of the mosaic: of the microsites — those spots in the forest that could start a fire, and those that could spread it: and those which would absorb and stop it, too. I look at diversities of vertical structure, and lateral structure, in unlogged country; at species mix. In the Yaak especially, due to its unique diversity, there are amazing bands of change on every mountain. You move through a forest of old lodgepole and then, going fifty or a hundred feet higher, into a forest of fire-buffering cedar, or cedar-hemlock. Then the slope will flex more sharply, will cross to a southern aspect, and you find yourself in a grove of fire-promoting ponderosa pine, and at the top of that ridge, fire-resistant old growth Douglas fir.

I'm learning to look at *nature*.

Sometimes I think that it is the wolves who are helping, aiding and abetting, joining the resurrecting fires in the West: or not the wolves, but rather, the absence of them. I noticed it just the other day. I was planting some young cedars and had put up gated slats and screens around them to keep the deer, elk and moose from browsing them in winter. (I keep the enclosures around them until they get tall enough to be above the browse line.)

I began planting the trees a couple of years ago. And it just hit me this spring: the before-and-after of it. I haven't been seeing any young aspens anywhere in the woods — just big ones, thirty and forty and fifty years old — trees born back in the days of predators — and I noticed too that in my enclosures the aspen sprouts are doing great, but only in my enclosures. The deer herds are increasing so steadily and dramatically that they're eating all the young aspen and perhaps cedar. The cedar, especially, are fire resistant, because they help cool the forest, which helps retain moisture — which helps buffer fires.

There are too many deer — or rather, not enough predators. They are perhaps near the edge of stripping the woods bare — changing the composition of the forest over the past fifty years, in ways as subtle as our ways have been offensive and immense. The ways of rot versus the ways of fire.

It is not just the wolves, of course. It is everything; it is all out of balance.

It was a good snow year, this year. By April we were already watching the sky like farmers. But the snow and rain mean little. A greenhouse-hot summer followed by a lightning storm, followed by a windy dry day — everything can change, and will change; if not this year, then next. For this reason, and so many others, we need to keep the untouched wilderness cores — the untouched roadless areas in each national forest. They act as buffers, absorbing and diffusing the spread of huge hot fires throughout the West. They're better at putting out fires, or diluting them, than ten thousand or one hundred thousand Marines — better than a billion-dollar-a-year effort. Every forest needs a big wilderness area — a chain of dedicated roadless areas, in perpetuity — come hell or high water, come war or peace, come world's end or world's beginning.

Call it a place to run to when things go wrong. When the whole rest of the world goes up in conflagration.

We're just now learning new things in the West. We're always learning new things: things known by people before us, old civilizations, but now forgotten.

We scan the hot western skies in August for signs of approaching storms and try to detect the feel of electricity in the air. Any breeze at all can feel ominous. We are remembering another of nature's rules: Payback is hell.

My Congressman

THE SUMMERS ARE SO BRIEF and the winters so long up here. I love it.

In the first week of 1996 — another reelection year — Pat Williams surprised everyone by announcing that, like so many other congressmen and congresswomen, he would not seek reelection.

For a long time he had spoken of how rough and unrewarding the work had gotten, how futile. The gridlockers and obstructionists working at the corporations' beck and call could stop anything good, anything noble. That was wearying to him, he said, plus there was this: he missed Montana. The last time I saw him (at a rally for his '94 reelection) he and his wife, Carol, talked about their simple dream of one day having a garden like the one they used to have before they went to Washington.

Whether parrying or thrusting or counterpunching, he was a champion. He fought for the arts, for education, for the environment, and for the rights of women and workers. In this respect, you could call him a liberal: he was for the freedom of things, not the enslavement of them. There are several individuals in Washington who accumulated the kind of power he had there, but unlike many of them, Williams did not lose his compassion as he gained that power.

We hear so much raging about the government. I wonder how many other citizens will ever have the bittersweet, mixed good fortune to lament so deeply the retirement of one of their senators or representatives. You don't hear much about that kind of thing any more.

He and his family were in Washington for roughly a fifth of a century. Hell yes, they deserve a garden back in Montana. Hell yes, they deserve to once more observe the cycles of their home. And a thank-you letter, too, if you don't mind.

I don't know who, if anyone, will step up to take his place. And we need to be spending our postage and passion, our letters and envelopes, on those who still pull the levers. But he was such an honest and square force, such a one-man counterbalance to the excesses and greed of industry, that there is no way I can pass up the opportunity to say thank you. And any protection that in the future will come to the Yaak — any protection of the wilderness — will be laid on the cornerstone of his work, his sweat, his values. He stood up for the Yaak when no one else would. I don't know how long it will be before we see his kind again, if ever.

Hot Lead

THE CANDLE BURNS at both ends. There are small groups of environmentalists and loggers throughout the West, and even down in Libby, who in recent years, bloodied by battles of the heart, have begun trying to get together in order to come up with solutions. There are very few people, if any, out there who work in the woods — sawyers, log-truck drivers, timber cruisers, tree planters — who want to see injury done to the land.

In the Yaak, it is getting harder and harder to ignore what has been done to the land — and what is still being done.

The shareholders of the big corporations — the ones who never see the land — are the only ones who do not care. Sometimes I wake up in the morning not with the peace-of-mind with which I like to begin a day's work, but with anger — with the image of men and women opening their morning papers to check the daily stock quotes on these corporations of whom they own shares. *They do not care.*

So we've been having these meetings, these dialogues, where we discuss dreams, desires and hopes, right next to the context of next week's mortgage payment — or last month's past-due one.

Part of the problem in attitudes — in the tenseness of hearts between those who fight for the last wilderness, and those who fight to erase it — is one, as I perceive it, of a strange mixture of guilt and pride, on both sides of the argument.

Few people want to accept at a conscious level the notion that what their employers have done is wrong. How can it be wrong if such serious good has come from it — if it has helped put food on the plate, has helped raise a family? This notion of wrongness, by unfair and unfortunate association, could easily imply, across a short leap of logic, that the workers were being judged as being wrong-hearted. The workers might badmouth their employer in private, but will almost always set up a wall of defense against criticism from the outside.

Along these lines, comments that often come out of our meetings (which are sometimes heated, but not as much as you'd think — we're neighbors, after all; we all know by this point each other's quirks and stances — we know which buttons not to push, and know also when the bullshit's getting a little deep) include the complaint by resource-extraction folks ("loggers") that while they realize there have been abuses in the Yaak in the past, they feel like the environmentalists take pleasure in "rubbing our noses in it."

Of course we think that this is a misperception on the loggers' part. What the environmentalists would *really* like to be doing is what anyone else would like to be doing — working a garden, spending time with family, hunting, fishing, reading a book, watching a show. . . .

But what's encouraging about comments like these is that, even only a few years ago, rather than complaining about the nose-rubbing, there would instead have been complete and total denial that the wilderness, and surrounding forest, was in any state of disrepair whatsoever.

It's hard — nearly impossible — when your identity has been wedded (sometimes across generations) to the timber industry. The line can be so fine between one's employer and one's self that criticism of the company becomes criticism of your own values and identity. It's been one of the recipes for war, throughout history. Of course it must feel to the loggers as if we — the environmentalists, and even the public-at-large, won't ever let up: that we're always going to be criticizing the past, and that we are unwilling to accept the hope that big timber can ever do anything right.

On the other hand — from this side of the battle (and if both sides are losing, then who, might we ask — knowing the answer — is winning?) — the environmentalists feel like if we don't speak up critically against the past, it will become accepted — as it once was when there was plenty of wilderness to go around.

And where environmentalists are coming from, as well, is a position of distrust so deep-rooted in truth and history that the distrust approaches and sometimes crosses over into panic. The Forest Service, as well as the timber industry, like any political organism caught red-handed, is *always* saying it's changing, that it's going to get its act together. Their most effective form of attack, they've found out, is to get the public to let its guard down.

Industry will kick in a hundred bucks, or a thousand, to some community need. Industry will talk about all those little piss-ant seedlings they planted. And they keep making sure, with those profits, that their puppets get elected to office.

The meetings are good. It's hard enough to dislike someone you don't know — harder still to dislike someone you're having a dialogue with. Our dreams are so fantastic — sometimes more surreal than fiction, lying square in the middle of what seems logical and pragmatic, but is really at the far edge, for the time being — or beyond the far edge — of political reality.

Still, sipping coffee late into the night, we continue to have these dreams, and talk about them. We talk about what the woods mean to each of us, and are comforted to find that about 80 percent of it is common ground. It's good, after a while, to know where each other stands, and to be able to speak freely about our passions. It feels like bullet-making, these plans — or rather, the precursor to these plans — these dreams of the future. It feels as if we are converting ourselves — *spending our lives in this battle* — to hot lead and then pouring ourselves into the molds of our making, the molds of our dreams. *Yes, we need timber. Yes, we must stay out of roadless areas.*

What if the corporations could no longer run amok on the public lands; what if they could no longer milk freely (or with our subsidies, our blessings) the public wildlands? What if they could be driven from the region — and with it, the malarial specter of their legacy, now ingrained into western communities and cultures, of boom and bust?

For eight, nine, ten million dollars, we could buy one of the old abandoned mills along the railroad tracks and show the forest products industry how it's supposed to be done: certified sawyers working selective cuts — no more clearcuts — and rather than shipping raw logs to distant mills, we could use one-tenth the volume of wood, or one-one-hundredth, in a value-added local industry, rather than hurling ourselves down the steep hill, in these last few remaining years. . . .

Each year, the bare gullies, the gouges of eroding soil, cut deeper and deeper, up on those high-elevation clearcuts: up at the source of wildness. I cannot look at them without feeling physically — not emotionally, but physically — the sensation of injury. I cannot shut my feelings out to that numbness any more. I have become too much of this place.

Such is our tiny progress that I can say these things to my logger friends, and they will listen respectfully; as I will listen to them and feel frustration — though not responsibility — when they talk of wood they want to cut but can't bid on or how they can't be competitive against the multinationals. Many of them are struggling monthly to make huge payments on big machines they bought on interest and promise back in the high-volume days of Champion's quick and calculated forest liquidation frenzy. The machines have to be used, to pay for themselves, and some of them run a quarter of a million dollars each, new. But many of these machines could be used in restoration projects, and salvage projects.

And I keep pointing to the far hills — to the last wall of unroaded blue ridges — Roderick, Saddle, Gunsight, Pink Mountains — and saying, I want to know that in each valley we will set aside untouched cores, untouched places, that will always be managed only by God-as-nature, against which to measure those other areas managed by man-as-God. I do not want to take it all, I want to give back instead to the wilderness some of that with which we have been entrusted and bequeathed.

We talk late into the night about the things that could be done with the wood, the care that could be given to it — Yaak Valley bookshelves, or specialty beams, or siding; a glue-lam plant, where bark and sawdust and limbs and small, crooked trees could be compressed to make building materials. . . . Furniture, or cabinet-making; a finger-joint molding plant. . . . Any of fifty wood-products industries that could be sustainable to both the human community and to the land, rather than pursuing to the bitter, tragic end, the last dying gasps of this century of liquidation that is finally drawing to a close. . . .

Some of them — the CEOs — want it *all*. And they don't care what happens to the communities that are left in the wake.

Champion International's exodus from this area was a good example. They were here in the '70s and '80s; they clearcut almost all of their lands in the Yaak (this served as a double whammy, as they owned mostly riverbottom lands — prime wildlife habitat). They clearcut their inventory to raise cash to defend against corporate raiders, and to hide or erase their capital. This sent an unsustainable, artificially high volume of wood through the local mills, which hired a great deal of short-term help to handle the glut (and depressed prices, spurring demand). Champion quickly ran out of their own timber, of course, and then put the squeeze on the Forest Service (through the industry-elected representatives and senators) to let Champion cross over onto the national forests and continue to cut at or near the same high rate as on the public lands. One of the rationalizations was that no one wanted to see all those people lose their jobs — and Champion kept saying that right on up until the day they left town and took their operations to the southern United States, where trees grow faster and where, critics said, they had planned to go all along.

And on their way out of town, they divided up all their clearcut lands into ten- and twenty-acre ranchettes — a couple thousand acres' worth in a single year — the social and biological equivalent of a firebombing. The Rocky Mountain Elk Foundation, Ruffed Grouse Society, Land and Water Conservation Fund, Nature Conservancy and other similar organizations never had a chance. *Cash flow*; one-time quarterly profits. The sad thing is, if they'd tried, they could have gotten as much money, or more tax credits, by selling the land in larger biological units rather than the mass fragmentation.

In the old days, our arguments would now take this tack: Well, Mr. Environmentalist, sounds like you get yours, but you don't think anyone else should get theirs.

It's true that I put my life in hock for the next twenty years to buy the land I'm living on — that I outbid a man who intended to clearcut it and then resell it, for subdivision — and that it is a lot of land, to my way of thinking. It is land that I intend to take care of, to log selectively and be passionately respectful of. And it is not the people moving onto the ranchettes that alarm me, for I have no right to judge them. It is the volatile manner in which all the land was dumped on the market that I judge. The shock to the system. The disrespect of the corporation to both the human and biological community in which it had been operating (and profiting) those many years.

A supple, healthy system can absorb dramatic fluctuations — can withstand volatility. But an injured or fragmented one is less supple, and takes longer to heal — and must be treated more respectfully. I think it's going to take a long time to protect the last wilderness of the Yaak, and that by the time people finally agree that those last corners need protecting, those areas will be gone.

In the meantime, we can try to build, or recover, respect for the place. I believe that is the first and most important step. We'll start small. Small and true.

We dream on, in these meetings. What if we could set up a local corporation that would be comprised of the community's loggers and environmentalists — not that the two are necessarily different, or have to be — and could have project areas on the National Forest (outside of the last roadless areas) that would be dedicated to selective harvest; what if bids on salvage sales — dead and dying lodgepole and other species, rather than live green sales — could be weighted competitively toward those operators, those sawyers, who rated the highest on performance evaluations made by their peers?

What if, instead of subsidizing, to the tune of one to two billion dollars per decade, entry into these fast-diminishing roadless areas, some small fraction of that monstrosity could go toward job creation geared at reclaiming, for fish and wildlife and forest health, those lands injured in the past — and the lands which are being injured, even at this moment?

In 1992, on the Kootenai (Yaak's) National Forest, timber harvest lost taxpayers approximately $20 million; in 1993, $2 million; and in 1994, $1.4 million. (Harvest levels went down each year, too; it doesn't take an Einstein to figure out that the less timber that was cut, the less money was lost.)

There *are* jobs in the woods, jobs left in the forest; and we can make there be even more of them, if we don't blow it. But they will be there only as long as the forest is there — only as long as the forest is healthy and supple, relatively unfragmented. The rancher and writer Ralph Beer tells of a funny (at the time) line uttered to him by A. B. Guthrie, author of the classic *The Big Sky*, concerning the exodus of people coming to Montana to get a glimpse of nature, and who had a blood-craving to see real and healthy cycles once again — in their communities, and out on the land itself. "They're all headed this way," Guthrie warned, "and every one of 'em's wearin' perfume." And, it might be added — if they have any backbone — registering to vote.

Kathleen Norris hits on this same emotion of insiders-versus-outsiders in her excellent book *Dakota*, when she comments on how in many rural communities there is the joke that an "expert" is someone who's fifty miles from home. Again, it's funny. But such sayings, while offering the comfort of humor, also run the risk of nourishing a brittle smugness.

We'd better save these lands that mean something to us — those of us who live on them and know them — before someone who doesn't know them comes along and does it for us.

The system is no longer supple. Nothing "locks up" a wilderness more than a two-thousand-acre clearcut on a sixty-degree slope.

I've spent most of my time in these essays trying to celebrate the wild, rather than running down or disparaging the enemies of the wild: those who would tame and kill and sell and regulate everything, from art to grizzlies, poems to rivers. But sometimes snarls of dismay or outrage have arisen, in these essays — criticisms both direct and indirect. Big business-owned congressmen seem, in my mind anyway, to be most often in the line of fire, but so too, allowing the theft of wildness of the national forests, is the bureaucracy known as the United States Forest Service.

The paradox of these criticisms is like the one involved in criticizing big business: the system sucks, but not the individuals, the workers, within the flow (or suckhole) of the system. Almost to the one, they are men and women who love the woods and who are caught in a bad situation. And doubtless, after years and years, they're getting a little tired of my squawling and bellyaching — of me scratching words on the paper gotten from trees, asking, begging, pleading, shouting that we save the last special places for all time.

There are time clocks to be punched. After a while, you get so weary — and the system seems so immovable, so static — that you'd really rather just tune it out and look ahead to five o'clock and wonder *What's for supper?* and *Give it a break; give us a break.*

That said — that there are great and passionate individuals working in the Forest Service (which is responsible for nearly a tenth of all the land in the United States) — one of the heartbreaking obstacles we face, in trying to manage the forests prudently — and in trying to protect the last roadless areas — is the incentive clauses. Brad Wetzler describes the mechanics of the salary raises and cash bonuses sometimes given to supervisors of various national forests: "The more timber he sells, the more money he can spend on his forest and the more merrily his career spins along."

The performance incentives sound fine, but when excessive logging — clearcutting — and roadless entry factor into this cash-bonus equation, when both the laws of our country and the laws of intact nature are broken in pursuit of these goals of timber quotas (set by industry, via their puppet congressmen), it seems similar to a teacher's bonus that is based not on students' test scores but on how much havoc the teacher can wreak in his or her community.

Why not give cash bonuses for protecting wilderness, and for protecting the sustainability of local communities? For the recovery of an endangered species in a forester's region, rather than giving bonuses for making the list grow ever longer?

I suspect big timber multinationals will be active in the Northwest until the last trees are gone. Unchecked — much less aided and abetted by Congress — big business will eat the world. But what if the government could protect us from such raiders? Am I dreaming? Is it too much to expect of one's government?

Secretary of Labor Robert Reich, responding to AT&T's

infamous New Year's 1996 stockholder gift, laying off 40,000 employees, writes, "It has become politically fashionable to argue that movie studios and TV networks should avoid lewdness or violence, even though these dubious themes generate large audiences and fat profits. Well, what about a corporation's duty to its employees and its community? The sudden loss of a paycheck can be more damaging to family values than a titillating screen performance."

Globalization, and the electronic transfer of capital, is making the notion of community meaningless to most corporations — and with increased competition, the leaning and meaning of America, corporate executives, writes Reich, "claim, with some justification, that they have no choice." Investors demand ever-increasing quarterly profits; and then when one corporation merges or melts down, the investors wire their money over to another corporation.

Reich suggests that "If we want profitable companies to keep more employees on their payrolls, or place them in new jobs that offer similar wages and benefits, or upgrade their skills, or share more of the profits with them or remain in their communities, we will have to give them an economic reason to do so.

"Perhaps the benefits of incorporation should be reserved for companies that demonstrate such responsibility. Alternatively — and more realistically, in these parched political times — perhaps corporate income taxes should be reduced or eliminated entirely for companies that do so.

"Don't blame corporations and their top executives," Reich concludes. "They are behaving exactly as they are organized to behave. If we want them to put greater emphasis on the interests of their workers and communities, society must reorganize them to do so."

We are all complicit. Shareholders pour gallons of fuel into the maw of the beast, but as consumers, we are almost constantly, daily, checking the oil and changing the wipers — helping to keep the giants in such good running condition.

We may have the briefest spat of a boycott, once in a blue moon, as with Exxon, or Union Carbide, but for the most part we keep on breeding, consuming and forgiving — breeding, consuming and forgiving beyond thought, reason or balance. We know we are at the edge of the last of the public wildlands — we know there are no more — but we do not turn back, we do not turn away: almost as if we feel powerless to do so. As if we are afraid that big business will get angry at us if we clamor that they do so. As if big business owns us, rather than the other way around.

We are all complicit. We live in wood homes, we burn wood, we read and write books etched on the skin of trees. The heft of a phone book in your hands as likely as not comes from the fast-disappearing virgin rain forests up on the coast of British Columbia. *Are telephones bad?* No. We are all complicit.

It is our very complicity, however, that gives us the right — the responsibility — not to be silent, but to speak up. We have to begin putting the brakes on. We're hurtling down the rapids, with big business at the throttle, grinning a mad grin for history.

We are the ones who have let it get taken this far — all the way to the edge. It is our duty to speak up, and to stop at the edge of that which we have allowed to go so far.

It's obvious I love the place. Less obvious, perhaps, that I love the people who live here. There's a deadly dull and dry section of the story I have to tell here, one of mind-numbing criminality and excess. No one wants to hear the kind of story I have to tell next: no one. Simple eco-rant; simple math. But I must tell it, because it is my home.

In 1995, the Republican-dominated Congress, reading the invisible ink they used to draft the Contract on America, passed a bill called the Salvage Logging Rider. The bill, written by the timber industry, would eliminate environmental appeals of illegal logging in the national forests. It stated that it would apply only to "salvage" logging — traditionally the term is used to refer to the harvest of trees that are already dead or dying. But in the bill, industry lobbyists expanded the definition to include any and every tree in the forest.

The bill was tacked on to the end of the 1995 Budget Rescissions Bill. President Clinton vetoed it, but then a month later changed his mind and passed it, in the summer of 1995.

Not just the Yaak, but a hundred other valleys across the West, began to crumble. A place that was already hanging by a thread was exposed to a savage lawlessness, perhaps undreamed of even by the greediest bureaucrats.

Free of the restraint of laws and regulations, the Forest Service moved quickly, planning six salvage sales in roadless areas on the Kootenai that will log more than 10,000 acres, and which will build and rebuild more than 138 miles of road. One clearcut that is scheduled will reach a size in excess of 1,700 acres. Prime grizzly bear recovery zones will be entered. Knapweed and other noxious invasives will follow these new roads into the wilderness, displacing the native grasses that elk rely upon: weeds spreading into these logged areas like wildfire. There are at present eighteen clearcuts planned that are in excess of what used to be the maximum allowable limit of 40 acres per clearcut.

Kim Davitt writes, "The Kootenai National Forest has become a regional horror story. Approximately 60 percent of all the salvaged timber scheduled for harvest in Montana comes from the Kootenai. Environmental organizations believe that the cost [to taxpayers] may exceed $1 billion."

Late summer 1995, Gunsight Mountain in the Yaak. Steve Thompson, the northwest field organizer for the Montana Wilderness Association, a volunteer, Susan LeValley, and I have gone up into the roadless area to investigate Forest Service claims that this area has been devastated by a nearly total sweep of high-intensity fires. We have the Forest Service maps in hand — the ones that show where all the clearcuts are planned.

It's a lovely August day. You can feel autumn lying just

ahead: a week or two away — maybe three weeks. But soon. Flickers move through the woods ahead of us. It's been only a year since the fires moved through here. But the undergrowth is green and lush. The *vaccinium* bushes — many of them chest-high — hang heavy with purple huckleberries. Moving up an old game trail, our clothes soon become stained purple from brushing against the ripe berries, and our hands and faces soon take on the purple coloration as well. It's a cool morning. There's a lot of wildlife sign — deer, bear, moose, elk.

We stop often, and examine the maps: believing them at first, and then unable, but still trying to believe them — repositioning them, trying to give the Forest Service the benefit of the doubt — but it soon becomes evident to us that the maps are, at best, simply erroneous. Up near the ridge, for example, we do finally find a stand that has burned intensely, as the map indicates, but this could not be one of the stands slated for harvest — the trees are all only about twelve feet high and as thick around as your wrist. They are overstocked — growing too close together — which is one reason they burned, and burned hot.

We move higher, to the ridge itself, and then laterally, into the heart of what the Forest Service has labeled the red zone: the burn of greatest intensity. The landscape folds and twists — rock slopes, creeks, seeps, springs — and at times, even only a year after the fire, it is hard to tell there had even been one. Giant larch and fir tower above us, a lush cool canopy sending down a pleasing mix of sun and shadow: *old growth*. These are immense trees, and even more amazing, they are immense at an elevation of 6,000 feet. Sometimes you'll still find an occasional stand like this down on the valley floor, around 3,000 feet — but almost never this high, where the growing season's so much shorter, and conditions so much harsher. These giants have had it at least twice as hard, and have taken perhaps twice as long to grow to this size — and in the process, they have orchestrated an incredibly complex, earned place in the world — relationships that we do not understand yet, at this or any other elevation: the interplay of the thin soil, insects, pathogens, bacteria, temperature, moisture, wildlife and wildfire. We can feel the unnameable quality of this forest, however — its complexity. We can feel the difference. It is not subtle.

It's a zone of cool fire, if anything — patchy mosaics of charcoal lie beneath the lush green huckleberries, and occasionally we'll cross a zone of moderate intensity burn, where some young understory fir and thin lodgepole and spruce burned — but there certainly doesn't seem to be enough timber up here to justify building new roads up this steep rocky slope. Helicopter logging might work, perhaps — though we have seen better salvage sites down lower, in areas that have already had roads built into them. (At a meeting with the Forest Service they had explained that helicopter logging would not be economically feasible. I'm not extraordinarily naive, but I was shocked nonetheless: it was the first time I'd ever heard them admit so bluntly that they were in the business of managing the forests for the timber industry rather than for wilderness or wildlife qualities or the future. I'd never heard it discussed so openly. I guess that the fact that environmentalists were powerless to stop them due to the salvage rider is what elicited the confidence of truth-telling.)

We pass through a one-acre patch of hot burn — there are fifteen, maybe twenty good sawlogs standing — trees that are dead or will die. The ash is deep and the slope is very steep: if machines operate here, heavy erosion will surely occur. If the snags are allowed to fall on their own, however, landing downslope, wind-gusted, they'll act as small dams, strainers of sediment. They will prevent erosion; they'll hold the ash and fragile soil in place and allow new seedlings to regenerate.

We pass through a stand of the rarest of things: old-growth, high-altitude lodgepole that survived the fire. These trees have the genetics we need: they've survived beyond their years, avoided bug infestations, evaded the infamous fire of 1910, as well as this most recent 1994 fire. They've lived up here at the top of the world, immersed to the hilt in the glories of natural selection, and now we're going to erase all that work, all that grace, all that *meaning*.

The slopes are so steep. These giant trees clutch little pockets of soil. If we cut them once, at this elevation, there will not be enough soil, nor soil nutrients, for regeneration. I have seen too many other areas in the Yaak clearcut in places like this, and know what the results will be: permanent moon-scaping.

We stop by a creek that the fire burned across and gather a backpack full of fist-sized morel mushrooms, apricot-colored in the light. We sit, stunned, in a shaft of sunlight, on a newly burned log resting among the rocks. We try to believe that there has been some mistake: that we are on the wrong mountain; that the satellites got it wrong. The immense trees — many of them untouched by fire — sway above us.

We see movement below. Three men are moving through the forest, among the old giants, with cans of spray paint. We're surprised: we didn't know anyone else would be up here. We watch as they spray an occasional tree blue, indicating that it should be saved. The theory is that it will not be a clearcut if they have one or two healthy trees left behind — and that the remaining tree, or trees, will continue to drop seed cones, saving the expense and effort of tree-planting. Better yet, from the timber companies' point of view, the remaining trees will often increase seed production dramatically, in an effort to compensate for the sudden loss of all the surrounding forest.

The men do not see us. We watch them for a while, then announce our presence. "You missed some," Steve says, king of understatement. The men are churlish, sullen. They want to know who we are and what we're doing in the woods.

My inclination is to tell them that it is none of their damn business — that I'm a citizen out here on the public lands — but Steve tells them that he's a wilderness advocate and that he came out here to see what was going on.

"We've got to get to work," one of the men grumbles as they drift away — implying that we do not — and they move off, getting paid for being in the woods, for tearing down the wilderness, while we sit there, unpaid, watching the wilderness get torn down. They do not spray any more trees to be saved; they do not even look at the old giants. We know then that the bottom line, the answer to the equation, has been filled in by the timber companies — *we need this much wood from this sale for it to be economically feasible* — and they are merely juggling things to make sure that the answer, that volume, is achieved.

There's not a damn thing we can do. Except write books. Congress, and the president, has seen to that.

We gather huckleberries. We hike home — worried, sickened. The day blossoms beautiful around us, but further and further, what is being done to our home, and to our country, erodes and endangers our capability for joy.

I do not want to add up the hours I spend staring out at the disappearing forests and wildness, feeling troubled or saddened, agitated or angry. I do not want to know the sum of this loss.

Later in the fall, Steve coordinated a return trip to Gunsight, with representatives from the local forest service, the timber industry and the media. On that field trip, timber industry people agreed that the giant trees were actually more of a bother — almost too big for the mills to handle efficiently — and that often the value of such giants was merely to use as foundations on which to deck the other logs — stacking them in the mud — and to butt other logs up against, in the lumber yard. Steve Thompson wrote that no one on the field trip — Forest Service personnel included — suggested that any of the old-growth larch and fir trees would die from the Gunsight fire.

On behalf of the Montana Wilderness Association, Thompson wrote an editorial criticizing the proposed massive clearcut in this, and other roadless areas in the Yaak and elsewhere. A Forest Service official rebuked MWA, admonishing critics of the salvage logging rider to "go out on the ground

. . . and see the reality." And the Republican senator from Montana, Conrad Burns, told a radio audience in Billings that salvage logging covered by the rider takes only timber "that is on the ground."

"Ironically," Thompson writes, it is the Forest Service official "who has refused to see the reality on our national forests. Twice MWA has invited him to join us on field trips to see his agency's plan to clearcut green, healthy timber in roadless areas. And twice he has demurred or ignored the invitation, preferring instead to defend the indefensible from his Missoula office."

Thompson writes, "The Gunsight Mountain clearcuts would violate the forest service's own standards for protecting wildlife habitat. This sale is opposed by the Montana Department of Fish, Wildlife and Parks because of the impact it would have on wildlife security and hunting opportunities" — chiefly elk, which require large secure roadless areas. "This opposition attracted the ire of the Montana Wood Products Association, which said that instead of protecting roadless areas, the elk-hunting season should be made shorter."

The Montana Wilderness Association's executive director, Bob Decker, wrote to the Forest Service official who refused to come to the Yaak and who criticized MWA's stance on wilderness and salvage logging: "MWA believes that salvage logging has a place on public lands in Montana. That place is defined by gentle terrain and stable soils, and it is accessible from existing roads. Emphasis should be given to small sales to local operators, and salvage operations should be completed in phases. Salvage projects should not entail clearcuts, but leave, as a rule of thumb, at least 30 percent of trees in every salvage unit."

Again, the organization is fighting for wilderness on one hand and for community and sustainable, independent economies on the other. They're burning the candle at both ends. They're not trying to obstruct — they're trying to create solutions and repair damages. If a way of life is preserved in the

Yaak and northwest Montana, I think it is largely MWA who will deserve credit for keeping the woods that loggers, hunters and wilderness-seekers alike share.

In April 1996, the proposed Gunsight sale was finally canceled by the forest supervisor after consultation with the United States Fish and Wildlife Service, who confirmed what we'd been saying: it would harm the elk and grizzly habitat. Other areas in the Yaak, however, were not so fortunate.

The Forest Service official's refusal to visit the Yaak; the disparity between what is said and what is done; between what is mapped and what is out there or not out there — *ground truthing.* I wake often thinking of the fights of local conservationist Chip Clark. Through information obtained under the Freedom of Information Act, Chip and others discovered that the Forest Service, when reporting to Congress how much mature timber was left on the Kootenai, claimed that 40 percent of the clearcuts contained mature timber. The real number was zero. But based on the hyperinflated figures — the "phantom trees," as they came to be known — Congress, the United States Fish and Wildlife Service, and Forest Service officials allowed a larger cut from the Kootenai.

On his own time and at his own expense during an Environmental Impact Statement review, Chip prepared his own alternative to present to the Forest Service, a plan that would have allowed them to cut even more timber than their own plan but that would have been comprised of mostly dead and dying lodgepole. Chip used his computers and extensive on-the-ground knowledge to meticulously catalogue, stand-by-stand, which volumes could have been cut from which area, and when and how. Chip's plan would have provided more wood and, ultimately, more jobs.

No matter. The agencies refused to even consider his work — the citizen's alternative, the conservationist's plan. They went ahead with *their* plan, which called for more road building into roadless areas.

Chip is in Costa Rica now, starting a new life.
I do not want to add up the hours.

Up to a quarter of a million loaded log trucks are scheduled to
roll out of the Yaak in the next couple of years. I've been
watching them roll, one after the other. The trucks all have
Idaho plates, not Montana plates, and if any of them have any
burned logs on them, I haven't seen them yet.

Still, we continue to attend meetings whenever they spring
up. We stake out our common ground, loggers and environmentalists, in-betweens and crossovers. The meetings don't
mean a damn thing to Congress, or to the Forest Service, or
to the multinationals, but we keep going to them. They have
all the durability of spider webs. But hopes and dreams will
not go away. We pour ourselves into the mold of them, even if
only in our imagination. "In dreams begins responsibility,"
Delmore Schwartz wrote.

The Forest Service official himself has mentioned the
Goethe quote, about dreams having magic and boldness in
them.

Where is the wilderness going? What happens to us when it is
gone? Are we richer, when this happens — are we more secure?

Will we know more joy, more peace?

The Totem Pole

IT'S SPRING, and I've been edged into occasional depressions. The assault on the environment — all the taking, instead of giving, near this, the end of our century of taking — has pushed me in the way that earth is sometimes pushed by bulldozers. I've given it — the letter-writing, the scheming and strategizing, the campaigning — my all. And it's taken it, my all, and changed nothing, it seems. It has cost me peace.

The greed of various politicians has led them to exuberantly court corporate lobbyists, and in 1994 these groups spent millions in public relations against the environment. It surprises me in the way it would surprise me to suddenly slip on ice. *I didn't know so many of us could be this wrong.*

I circle back, though, always, to my original thought, which is, People just don't know. The fight, after all, is going on in the backcountry. Nobody would vote for these things if they knew about them.

Given the short period of time we have here, how can anyone want to do anything other than good?

The geese out my cabin window have been spending great stretches of time sitting idly, or so it seems, in the open parts of the marsh. Floating but not moving, as if anchored, they seem to be watching and waiting — evaluating something. They've been sitting still for days, looking south.

*

This morning my neighbor from seventeen miles away came by so we could go look for a tree that he can carve and whittle and sand into a totem pole. It has to be just the right tree, taken early from the cycle of rot, regeneration and growth, and from a place where there are other felled trees. We didn't find one but we'll keep looking.

We went over the design of the creatures my wife and I want on the totem pole, and where we intend to place it: at the edge of the marsh in a forest so thick that tree branches will help hold it up. An almost secret place, where it would be helpful to know it was there in order to see it: a place where soft morning light will strike it, a place of dampness and shadow. A place of extraordinary lushness, where the totem pole itself can stand, slowly rotting and in that manner lowering itself back into the soil from which it came: but standing, like art, for a few years — for fifty or even a hundred years.

We sketched out several animals: the creatures that use the marsh, of course — the citizens of this place. Moose, geese, ducks, deer. A lone wolf. A bear near the base of the pole, while bears still exist in the world. A raven, an owl and, curiously, a heron, though there are no herons in this marsh, as there are no fish. It's a higher-elevation marsh up above the river, perched at the edge of a fault block, sitting one hundred feet above the river. It used to be a lake and I'm certain that when it was, fish were in it, and that there were herons too. And what would someone think, were they to find the rotting remains of the cabin and the totem pole: that this cabin was once by a lake where there were fish and herons? Or that the totem-maker did not understand the world around him, did not pay attention?

The paired-up ducks stay close to the geese, as if for protection, but perhaps only companionship. Sometimes I think the geese are just resting — both from the exhaustion of the long trip here, and in preparation for the one that lies ahead, only five or six months away. I try to drink in the beauty, the grace, of the mere and miraculous sight of them — as if they are a thing that is here only for the moment — *only this moment* — and that if I do not see it now, drink it all in and feel it now, it will be gone, taken away.

I have to make peace with my art and my anger, with our lives and their brevity — and yet, for me, it still involves fighting, and I will never give any of this up willingly, nor do I understand how any of us can.

I keep staring at the sunlit throats of the geese: the black eye masks, the elegant hoods.

Now comes the part I like: the south winds of April waving the shadows of bare branches across the yellow wood of the cabin, the dried catkins from last fall waving on the ends of the alder branches, the loyal creak and tick of the stove, and the muscles of my young bird dog shining chocolate as he prowls the straw-colored edges of the marsh, sniffing the dead, scent-filled grasses of last autumn. The songs of wood thrushes and black-capped chickadees, first back in the spring. I want to be a bird dog, a father, a stone man; a carved log back in the shadows, in the embrace of trees. I want that kind of strength — that kind of strength-in-decay. I dare not mourn so much that I forget why and how to live.

Metamorphosis

Dear Bill,

I'm sorry I missed you when I called two days ago, the day of the summer solstice. I left a message saying that I was going to take a hike for you. This may have sounded puzzling or imprecise but I didn't want to leave a long and windy message. Instead, I went up to the mountain that I climb every time I hear a friend is sick. I have been climbing it for eight years now and it has a success rate of 50 percent. I don't know if it was a holy mountain to the Indians or not. It is to me. Let me report to you what I saw on your hike.

It was a damp, rainy, foggy day. In clear weather you can see Idaho to the west and British Columbia to the north from the mountaintop, but I knew that would not be the case this day. I started up the trail midday. I had not been on the mountain all year — not since early last winter. There had been waist-deep snow, then; now the trail was overgrown with ankle-deep ferns and flowers. Seeps and springs glistened from the sides of the mountain, as if it were leaking, or bleeding, life.

I wound my way steadily, quickly, up the trail through old cool forest, anxious to get into alpine country — the steep grassy places where the mountain tips sharply skyward. Up there, I'll find the avalanche fields, where most tree seedlings get swept away by each year's snowslides — the mountain sheds the snow, and its trees, like skin, which leaves behind its core and essence: bare gray slickrock that shines in the sun. Clumps of rich soil — and tall grasses — cling wherever they can beneath the bright rock. This is the part of the mountain I am always most anxious to get to: the part where I feel things begin to happen.

The sky was slate-purple, luscious with rain — the clouds still bulging with storm, though it had been raining steadily for seven days already. It's the greenest I've ever seen the valley.

I hadn't been hiking for more than two or three minutes when I heard the chain-saw sound of an approaching plane — a small single-engine plane, such as the biologists use to chase and keep tabs on the grizzly bears they've live-trapped and fitted with radio telemetry collars. There are ten or twelve grizzlies in this valley — and four of them have collars. Ten or twelve doesn't sound like very many, and it isn't — there used to be one hundred thousand of them in the West, or even more. The bears in this valley are generally considered more valuable from a genetic standpoint due to their unaltered wildness than those few hundred bears that are left in Yellowstone and Glacier National Parks.

There's a big monster of a bear that hangs out on top of this mountain: a sweetheart, terrified of human beings, but big as a dinosaur. He *is* a dinosaur, holding on to his world with all four paws. I've seen him but once though I've seen his tracks often. His feet are as big as snowshoes. I was discouraged when I heard the tracking plane, not so much for the disruption of my solitude, but for the bears'. This big bear isn't radio-collared, but there must have been one up here that is — maybe a female. It's about that time of year when they get together.

A wonderful thing happened, though, before the plane could reach the mountain. The purple, silver-streaked storm clouds that were lingering on the back side of the mountain came drifting — *rolling* — over its crest, just as the little plane came near, so that it had to turn around before it reached the alpine fields where the grizzly often grazed.

So I knew he, or he and another one, was up there. But

now it was just he and I, or he, his radio-collared paramour and I; we had the mountain to ourselves.

I don't know what it is about this mountain that makes it special. And I don't want to know.

The pitch of it, once up into the avalanche section, the swept-clean slopes, demands everything your lungs have got. The slope sets your calves to burning, and after a while turns your upper legs to quivering jelly rather than sound muscle. It's an alchemical transformation. When you stop to rest, your heart feels like thunder. Even on a cold day, you're bathed in sweat by the time you're halfway up.

It's so damned good to be healthy.

I've seen almost every species of mammal in the valley up on this mountain, at one time or another. Often I see them in conjunction with each other.

None of this has a direct bearing on my report to you: this explanation of past trips. This hike for you was taken solely in the context of the present: only the present. I shall try to confine my remarks to what I saw, that day — not to what I didn't see, or had seen in the past.

I moved up into the clouds. My God, the names of all the flowers — hundreds of species, it seemed, all of them spangled with rain. Each summer I tell myself not to take them for granted; each summer I promise myself that I will learn all of their names.

But each year, I learn only a few. It's a gradual process. Still, I have to believe that it will all add up. That one of these days, I'll know them all. Glacier lily, mariposa lily, penstemmon, bluebell. Bellflower, lupine, paintbrush, aster. Tiger lily, phlox, lady's slipper, balsamroot. Canadian violet. Northern bog rein orchid.

I moved carefully into the fog, grateful for the cold mist against my face: grateful it had chased the clattering plane away, and grateful for the steaming beauty it brought to the landscape, the grass- and rock-scape, now that I was out of the

forest. It was good to be on a mountain that had a grizzly on it
— one of the very few grizzlies living outside a national park
— though I worried a little that the plane might have pissed
him off, and that the bear might not at the moment be feeling
good will toward men.

The fog got thicker near the mountain's crest. A spooky
white fog — not swirls and whisps of vapors, but a near total
whiteout. It was like being in the belly of a cloud, which I
suppose I was. Ordinarily it would seem like I was at the edge
of danger, pushing beyond the prudent edge of a thing —
past respect — but I figured that I had some kind of permission or authority — yours, perhaps — and that, well, whatever happened was meant to happen: was meant to be relayed
to you, in this report.

Still, I have to say, I'm glad I didn't see the bear.

Not that anything on this earth could remotely compare
to what you're facing: you're at the edge of all there may ever
be. Maybe your illness will reverse direction, through either
reasons known or unknown, like animal tracks across new
snow.

If I were to come upon a grizzly bear, high up in this
cloud, walking down the ridge toward me, he or she would
probably only stop, squint and sniff at me, from whatever
close distance we encountered each other — grizzlies can
see about as well as humans, but have a sense of smell that is
about a hundred times better than ours — and then he almost certainly would have turned around and gone the other
way; as would have I — as would have I.

Things are far less certain, for you. Things are far more
dire.

So I was relatively unworried; only curious to see what the
mountain would show to me to report back to you.

A ghost-shape galloped past me, moving from right to left,
just at the farthest range of vision: a dark young bull elk, his
antlers in June velvet, running in a curious, steady, circus-
horse canter. A yearling; maybe a two-year-old. An adoles-

cent. I thought of your son, and your daughters, and pushed on. The elk slipped into the timber below.

Aside from walking a small circle for luck around the old stone cairn at the crest, I didn't spend much time there. It was my notion to cut a transect from east to west across the whole of this mountain, which runs long and narrow north-south; to dig deep, to reach into it not for all that it had but for all that it was willing to give you through me. I'd started at the headwaters of the creek on its east flank, climbed to the top, and now would drop down to the creek on its west flank — actually a high hanging hidden valley, almost like some place of the imagination; a perfectly green and serene spot. And then I planned to climb back up the steep west side, go over the top again, and down the east side, back to where I had started.

It would be like going fishing — like trawling with a wide net. I didn't know what I'd find or see for you.

It was raining lightly on the back side. Wood thrushes were singing. This reminded me of a book your company published, *Birds of Texas*, and in turn reminded me of another book you published, *Back Roads of Texas*. I remember us joking about doing *Back Roads of Montana*, and my horror at such an idea. It makes me laugh to think that now I am sending you a report and a description of my favorite place-without-a-road. An even deeper baring of the soul.

Descending the western side is especially refreshing because of all the deciduous leaf litter underfoot. There's still the Pacific Northwest coniferous overstory — larch, fir, spruce, lodgepole pine and white pine — the giant cedars lie farther below, where the water accumulates — but on this near-vertical descent there's an incredible abundance of not only ferns and forest flowers, but broad-leafed deciduous trees as well: maple, aspen, buffaloberry, huckleberry, alder, ceanothus, even sasparilla. It's a place where two worlds collide — or if not collide, where they get pressed tightly together right here at this edge, to form a new world.

The deciduous leaves seem to rot easier — seem, in their broadness, to trap and retain moisture more readily between themselves and the soil — and because of this, the soil is rich, thick and black. This is a young valley, just-sprung-up yesterday from the glacier's retreat; the trees, because of the Pacific Northwest weather systems, are huge, but the soil is thin: you cut the trees once, and they won't come back like they were before. Not until a new bedding of soil forms. Which — if the trees are left alone — might take a few thousand years.

This is the richest soil I've seen in the valley. The healthiest. Perhaps the way this side of the mountain faces the west-approaching storms causes it to catch more moisture: causes it to even create its own moisture. Perhaps the west-setting sun, warmer than the rising sun, has over time more thoroughly weathered and disintegrated the rock — dissolving it like geological fertilizer, to add to the mystery of the forest below. Perhaps. . . .

It is a healing mountain.

Yellow warblers and yellow tanagers fly past like creatures escaped from a lifetime of imprisonment, singing and swooping. The needles of the coniferous trees do not break down and return to the earth as easily, as quickly, as do the leaves of the deciduous trees. There's a beetle that helps chew up the waxy coating on some of these coniferous needles, however, thereby enabling the rotting process to get started, where otherwise it would not. They're vital to the process of soil formation, these chewing bugs — vital to the forest, vital to the sky, to life. They're one of the rare leaf-eating insects in the forest. I remember a friend telling me how most insects in this forest were predators — that they ate each other — because there were so many billions of them that if they ate plant matter, they would quickly strip the entire forest bare.

As we are now doing. But that is another story, and is secondary to the story of immediate life — though it is not secondary to the longer view of things.

It's like looking through binoculars, or a telescope; like looking through them backwards, where everything's tiny, and then looking through them frontwards, where everything — even the moon — is huge.

What this trip today is about is to just try and look at things the way they are.

An attempt to make a walk without a thought of tomorrow.

I make this hike when people are well, too; the beauty of these woods — these untouched woods — has plenty to offer me when all is well. It's not a place I come to only in times of the sickness of friends. But it — the walk, and the woods — takes on, or seems to imbue — as with the pulse of a breathing thing — even more meaning, and deliver more understanding, when experienced in the context of illness, the context of sorrow.

The woods provide.

Going down through the lush dripping understory, trying to pick a path, and barely able to see ahead through the chill fog-clouds, might be akin to your present grasp of things. Everything on this walk reminds me of and amplifies your condition. I want to tell you about it all. Though I have made this transect on numerous occasions, no one path is ever the same as the one before it, and this time I discover one of the most amazing larch trees I've ever seen.

It's not amazing in size, and especially not for a larch; some in these woods are almost like redwoods — three-and four-hundred-year-old trees large enough to drive a car through. What's amazing about this one — it's about fifty years old, is my guess — only five or six years older than you — is that it metamorphosed into three separate trees. It's not at all uncommon for a larch to have twin trunks, but I've never noticed one before that has three trunks.

More amazing still, these three trunks, each as thick as a man's waist, spiral around each other as they rise vertically toward the canopy, so far above. They coil not so much like a great tree trunk, but like a vine, or DNA; like a corkscrew, like serpents around a staff.

Ordinarily such an unusual tree would not survive in the chaos of the forest — or what we call chaos, but which is of course a constantly changing state of unrelenting order and complexity, unrelenting grace.

Ordinarily, a tree like this one — so out of the mold for a classic larch — would have been pruned by insects, lightning, ice storm, or wind. It would not have been allowed to channel that energy — frivolous energy — all that sunlight, all that photosynthesis! — into such a seemingly whimsical and most decidedly unlarchlike design.

But I looked at what surrounded it, and I saw how it had survived.

Trees of different species formed a circle around it — fir, aspen, lodgepole, even cedar. Their branches, as it was growing, must have helped to shelter and stabilize it, hold it up, as though they were friends, or at the very least — and in the sense of the word that I think we must turn to the woods to relearn — like community.

There was no way to look at the tree and not think of you, and of all the other things that mattered.

I guess I'm not a hard-core pagan yet — and may never be. I still like to stop at the edges of realism, and not travel too far over into the world of the symbolic. I still sometimes cannot help but hold on to the notion that what we see and understand is all there is: that we have run out of mystery. I know in my heart that's wrong, but still, nearly forty years old, I have trouble shaking that stone wall certainty, the milieu in which I've grown up — the idea that we've got it all figured out. "It" being everything.

If I believed — if I dared to believe — more deeply in the power of symbolism, and the immeasurable, unknowable power of myth and ritual, perhaps I would have climbed that DNA-twisted tree and sawed or chopped down one, or two, or all of the spiraling trunks — a strange effort, two thousand miles away, to bend back the spirals of your own DNA — to make them change course; to divert the path of destiny, the genetic markers laid out in your beginning cast-of-dice, charting in advance, so long ago, the path of your flesh.

Or perhaps not: perhaps even if I believed, or knew, that a tree in Yaak could be connected to a man in Texas, I would have left it alone, as I did; believing, as I do, that there can be just as much power, or more power, in restraint as there can be in the desire to shape, manipulate, alter and impose.

I walked on.

There were mushrooms everywhere and of every color dazzling the eyes, and vibrant lichens, on the wet boulders: lichens that were hundreds, even thousands of years old. The undergrowth of *vaccinium* — huckleberry bushes — already had their swollen green berries on them, just waiting to turn purple in August, to transfer their chlorophyll to straight high-octane sugar; waiting to be eaten, in August and September, by the birds drifting southward, and by the bears drifting back up to the high north slopes, as they prepared to crawl down into the earth for their deep winter's sleep.

It all reminded me of you. The bears — your life. The bull elk — your son. The birdsong — your heart, our hearts, all hearts, hoping. The sound of the spring creeks trickling down the steep walls of the mossy, forested mountains — your life, again, and all lives.

Sometimes they build roads into the virgin forests up here under the pretense of getting into trees — lodgepole pine, usually — that have been infested with mountain pine beetles, for which lodgepole is a host. It's an intricate, highly evolved cycle about which entire books have been written. Basically, though, pine beetles attack overmature lodgepoles, killing them, sometimes in large numbers, which then sets that dead or dying stand up for a fire — usually lightning-caused — the heat of which the lodgepole's cones can then use to be cracked open and reproduce.

Through the ashes of the fire, all of the forest's nutrients are returned to the soil — the flames open the seed cones for the next forest — and so it goes. The fire destroys large numbers of the beetle "epidemic," as well. The cycle of the forest rises and falls, in that manner, like piston-and-valve, or calliope music. Like the hands of a potter working clay.

What's strange about this forest is that none of its lodgepole pines — though they're mature ones, even overmature — have beetles in them. By any account, this mountain is a place of unsurpassed health, from the soil all the way up to the tips of the treetops. These lodgepoles are eighty-five years old, and without a pine beetle in sight. These lodgepoles have the genetics, and the magic, that future land-managers — though, good God, not the current crop, it seems — will be interested in.

I pick my trail downward through the thick forest toward that backside creek in the high green hanging valley. I've never been in that valley without seeing a cow moose. I don't know if it's the same moose every time or not.

I keep thinking about DNA — about the bends in it, the alterations, that can yield or summon cancer — a meltdown of the flesh. The paths that are charted for us from the beginning, versus those that are sometimes chosen for us by others: by pollutants, contaminants, carcinogens. I'd recently read a newspaper column by a timber industry lackey who was pooh-poohing the dangers of dioxin. Never mind that it's the second-deadliest carcinogen known to man, next only to plutonium (another element for which the timber spokesman had kind words). The largest emission of dioxin, he said, actually comes from the forest itself when it burns. Dioxin, he said, was something trees inflict upon us.

I guess he ran out of space in his column, or in his mind, maybe, or just forgot and left out the part that forest fires release dioxin because the dioxin has settled on the needles of conifers as a result of chlorine precipitation from industrial emissions.

God, I hope you can turn this thing around.

As I get lower and lower, closer to the creek, it begins to rain again. Massive larch trees, giant burned-out skeletons, stand sentinel-like and tell the story of the 1910 forest fire, which burned, off and on, for a distance of 250 miles, from Spokane to Kalispell, and whose smoke was visible as far away as Chicago. It was this fire — redepositing all of the forest's nutrients, rather than trucking them off and putting them on a ship bound for Asia — which laid the foundation for the immense forests of this valley. Not all the trees burned — some in the valley are five hundred years, even a thousand years old — but those that did burn gave birth to an incredibly rich and blessed place. They left more behind than what they came in with.

In the valley, we talk about the 1910 fire — the magnitude of which is probably a two- or three-hundred-year event — as if it occurred back in the most ancient corner of history; and in some ways — in the scale of you and me, for instance — I guess it was.

In 1910, you wouldn't have been born yet. In 1910, perhaps even your father and mother wouldn't have been born. Your grandfather would have been a young man then, strong in the world.

So much green, everywhere, lush and dripping and wet.

The rain falls lightly on the broad leaves of false hellebore, a plant that the Indians of the British Columbia coastal tribes hold in highest esteem for medicinal purposes. You can't eat it — it'll make you sick — but the smoke from the burning green plant can heal both your body and your spirit. I snap one off above the base, leaving the roots to regenerate, and put it in my daypack to mail to you. The rain makes a pattering sound as it strikes the broad leaves all around me — I'm standing knee-deep in a helleborine garden. The sound itself — unusual for this valley — is healing. As the rain knifes through the conifers' needles it makes a steady hiss. I'm very near the creek now, muddy and wet to my waist. A ruffed grouse is drumming nearby, courting, perhaps, working toward his second clutch of the summer, following the freak blizzard only two weeks ago, which extinguished a fair number of the spring's hatchlings, the first clutch.

Life, go on, go on. Go on.

Through the forest I catch a glimpse of a faraway mountain — four, five miles upstream, in the headwaters of this secret valley. A little road was built into the edge of this roadless country, farther up in those headwaters, during World War II — it was thought that we'd need to cut more wood for building more ships — but the war ended before those trees could be reached, and the road is invisible now, completely grown over with alder and pines as big around as your thigh. Up at the headwaters, there is one smallish clearcut, up at the source of things, like a blemish, a nick or a cut one might have gotten while shaving. The rest of this green forest — despite the nick's relative tininess — seems somehow poised against it; suffering it quietly, absorbing and absolving the tiny sight of it — but not unmindful of it: not forgetting that it is there.

I'm in dark, dense timber close to the creek now. It's wet, and I slip. I hear the thunder of something large running away from me, or toward, I can't tell which, at first.

Away.

More 1910-charred giant larch skeletons. They were several hundred years old before they burned. That's a rule of the West, and a rule of the world: if it doesn't rot, it burns.

It if dies, it's born again — as long as there's a soil base for it to return to. Orange mulch or gray-black ash, it makes no difference; it lives and dies in its home and then lives again. Even when the soil is washed away, it is not the end of things, because then the sun and frost and snow and rain begin to work on the exposed bedrock, crumbling it and kneading and pulverizing it through the millennia to make soil again.

It's good soil, here, in this back-side valley. I'll send you some. It feels good to be standing on it. There are a lot of stories buried within it. It supports so much life.

Over on one of the other mountains earlier this summer — up on one of the burned mountains, scorched black in places from last autumn's fires — the bluebirds and flickers were swarming in search of all the remaining insects. The birds' songs were beautiful in that black landscape of birth, and the bluebirds were flying chips of color and song. It all has to rot or burn, and there's only so much in the bank. Forgive me if I keep repeating the obvious: it just seems like such a revelation to me that in the end it is all the same, and that it is really the part leading up to either of those two ends that makes life so sweet for us.

Here is a feather from these woods. Here is an antler. Here is a stone, still light years away from becoming soil.

The ranger I talked to last year, when I went down to the Forest Service office to protest a road being built into this last forest, said, in response to a direct question by me, that No, he didn't consider this mountain any different from any other. They'd tried to come in here and cut last year, but a court appeal ruled against them.

Didn't matter. They came right back and proposed the same thing this year, only bigger.

The ranger said that no, he wasn't aware of any particular magic hiding out in this little valley, that it was no different from any other mountain in the valley.

He was full of shit.

"I'll put it into the record that your comments were considered," he said curtly, glancing at his watch.

Here is the creek, then: you emerge into a glowing green place — holly, maple, water-drip, moth-dance. The scent of roses. Mayflies rise from the virgin creek. Cedar trees two hundred feet tall shade the still waters of a beaver pond, drinking the clear water with their almost-ageless roots. A giant cow moose and her calf, seemingly no larger than a small dog, stand in the bright healthy lime-green of the marsh grass farther downstream. Sunshine illuminates them.

The creek is narrow; in some places you could vault across it. And across the creek lies more unroaded country, and the beginning of another mountain.

I dip my hands in the creek and splash its water on my face. I turn and start back in the direction from which I have come.

If you make it — if you pull out and turn this thing around — you and I will have to take this hike next year, or the next.

If you don't, I will send the map — the rough sketch of it — to your family, so that your children might someday see it.

This is the thing I wanted most to share with you.

The moose and her calf — frightened by my presence — splash across the creek and go into the forest on the other side. I start the climb back into the rainclouds.

The swatch of gold shining on the marsh remains, waiting, like the light of hope itself. Not like anything come down from the sky, photosynthetic life from the sun, but like something deeper and more permanent: like hope from the center of the earth, hope from the soil.

The hope of fallen, rotting trees.

Conclusion

I HAVE LEFT OUT too much description in this book. Fact has replaced poetry, and — despite my knowing better — desire has been allowed to become so taut as to become brittle, and even to snap — risking the result of numbness. In art, it has often been said, what you leave out is more important than what you put in — but here I didn't dare leave much out. I wanted to bear witness to the facts. I wanted to lay out my heart, forgoing art's great schemes. There's no cleverness to be found here, only rawness: like the roar of a saw, with wood chips flying.

I am not afraid of failing at a short story — at a work of fiction. But I am afraid of failing the valley; and I am afraid of failing my neighbors, my friends and my community.

I believe the simplest and yet most inflammatory belief of all: that we can have wilderness and logging both in the Yaak Valley.

It would cease to be the place it is without any more logging; but it will cease to be the place it is, as well, if the wilderness is lost. There is not a day that goes by that I don't worry about it, and wrestle with the solutions, the issues.

I am not afraid of the wilderness, and I am not afraid to dream and hope and work.

I OWE MANY THANKS for the help received in the telling of this story. Thanks, as always, to my editors — Camille Hykes, Harry Foster, and Dorothy Henderson — and to Melodie Wertelet for the book's design, to my agent, Bob Dattila, and to Russell Chatham for the cover's painting.

Thanks also for the support of other conservationists, too numerous to name, who have listened sympathetically and observed with their own eyes the story of Yaak, and to the Forest Service personnel who have offered not resistance but quiet encouragement for the protection of Yaak's roadless areas.

I am in deep debt to and hold much appreciation for Steve Thompson, formerly the Northwest field representative for the Montana Wilderness Association (P.O. Box 635, Helena, MT 59624 — please join) for his tireless efforts to keep abreast of goings-on in the Yaak, and for his expertise and unceasing activism.

Much mention is made in this book of letter writing. A fine place to begin lobbying for the Yaak's unprotected wilderness is with your own senators and representatives. Other key judges determining Yaak's future include the chief of the Forest Service (P.O. Box 96090, Washington, D.C. 20090), the secretary of agriculture (14th St. and Independence Ave., Washington, D.C. 20250), the regional forester (P.O. Box 7669, Missoula, MT 59807), the Kootenai National Forest supervisor (506 Highway 2 West, Libby, MT 59923), Gover-

190 · *The Book of Yaak*

nor Mark Racicot (State Capitol, Helena, MT 59620), and Montana's senators, Max Baucus and Conrad Burns (U.S. Senate, Washington, D.C. 20510). These people would, I'm sure, enjoy hearing from you, as would the president (The White House, 1600 Pennsylvania Ave., Washington, D.C. 20500) and the vice president (Old Executive Office Building, Washington, D.C. 20501).

A copy of this book has been delivered to each member of Congress and to the administration of the president.